zation and control, which it want...

More broadly, he is eager to do what he can to ease tensions among the European allies, in part to bring some sense of common purpose to the alliance and thus to strengthen his own position in direct negotiations with the Soviet Union.

Cordiality Is Expressed

Despite the conviction among American officials that the 78-year-old general's policies have done much to delay European unity, Mr. Nixon seemed determined to make his stay here on a cordial note.

In his welcoming remarks at Orly, General de Gaulle described Mr. Nixon's visit as an occasion for "joy and honor" for his part, President Nixon described France as America's "oldest ally" and "oldest friend" and added, in a nice ward to his exposure to the general's judgment, counsel, wisdom and experience.

Both Mr. Nixon and his host wore no overcoats and spoke without text. However, Mr. Nixon had a prepared text in his pocket, which was, if anything, more effusive than the actual remarks. The press text was printed, in fact, as leaders of the modern world think so broadly as you, Mr.

Continued on Page 3, Column 1

Agency Shop Won By Municipal Union

By SETH S. KING

Mayor Lindsay announced yesterday that the city had reached an agreement with a municipal employees' union that would require nonunion city employees to pay the union a "service fee" equivalent to the dues that union members pay.

The pact, the first signed with a municipal union here, was made with Hospital Local in 420 of the State, County and Municipal Employees Union, which represents 12,000 of the 16,500 employees in municipal hospitals.

The Legislature authorizes the agency shop, the way would the be open for all municipal employee unions under the jurisdiction of the Office of Collective Bargaining to receive payroll deductions from all civil service workers these unions represent.

Continued on Page 19, Column 4

of not guilty and plead guilty to all counts as charged," he told a startled court. "I want to dissociate myself from my counsel."

After a short argument with Superior Court Judge Herbert he would put him in charge. He continued that it was interrupting the trial was "essentially unchanged" and that he was restchanged" and that he was restchanged" and that he was rest...

The attending medical team acknowledged concern over the respiratory complication because of the general's age.

During the argument, Judge Walker told Sirhan in an angry voice.

"Has to Be Proved"

"That has to be proved in a court of law," Judge Walker answered.

During the argument, Judge Walker told Sirhan in an angry voice. However, Mr. Judge Walker finally denied Sirhan's request and, during a recess in his behavior, warned him that if he was not quiet he would have to be put in chains. "Few" he could be forced to wear a face mask.

The defendant's latest outburst came on the first day of the defense's case in the small, crowded courtroom on the eighth floor of the Hall of Justice.

School Grades Evaluated

When the afternoon session began shortly after 2 o'clock, pleading for a guilty verdict as a sign that citizens of the United States were beginning to fight against our economic trends in the 212 major metropolitan areas since 1960.

Mr. Garrison, who had contended that the assassination had been carried out by employees of the Central Intelligence Agency, was not in court when the nine white and three Negro jurors returned a verdict after making a 35-minute summation late last night.

Mr. Shaw, wearing a sad smile, shook the hand of each juror as he left the courtroom shortly after 1 A.M., New York time. He said the not guilty verdict was a statement late in the day.

At Assistant District Attorney, who had handed most of the per cent of the case to our calling this verdict to make known his sentiment.

that the former President's condition before 6 P.M.

Asked how much strain the pneumonia put on General Eisenhower's scarred and weakened heart, the doctors said, "Considerable."

The five-star general's heart healthy enough, as a result of his seven myocardial infarctions—serious damaging of the principal pumping muscles as a consequence of blockage of the heart's main artery.

This morning's medical bulletin, first announced at the Pentagon, said General Eisenhower had suffered some respiratory difficulty" due to the pneumonia in his lower right lung. It mentioned his

Continued on Page 17, Column 2

SHAW ACQUITTED OF 'KENNEDY PLOT'

Jury Out 50 Minutes After Summation by Garrison

By MARTIN WALDRON
Special to The New York Times

NEW ORLEANS, Saturday, March 1 — An all-male jury early today acquitted Clay L. Shaw of a charge of conspiring to assassinate President Kennedy. The jury deliberated about 50 minutes.

The verdict came quickly despite a courtroom speech by District Attorney Jim Garrison.

SOME GAINS FOUND FOR URBAN NEGRO

U.S. Report Shows Income and Education Improving

By PETER KIHSS
Special to The New York Times

Negro youths have been catching up to whites in school attendance. Negro men's earnings are past about matching those of white women in year-round jobs. And the rise in Negro family income has been faster than the whites'.

These are among the brighter nationwide findings reported in a special Bureau of the Census study of economic and social trends in the 212 major metropolitan areas since 1960.

But the study also shows gloomier findings for Negroes living in the central cities.

Negro men's earnings lag behind whites', as much as 16 to 35 per cent in various categories. Negro unemployment and under-employment was more than 22.7 per cent in 1960 to 30.4 per cent last year. And 39 per cent of Negro children lived in homes lacking at least one parent in 1960.

For New York City, the study had covered a sample of 266,000 families, whose total were at the poverty level in 1959 while 206,000, or 10 per cent, were at this level last year.

New York City's white poor number some 198,000.

Continued on Page 16, Column 6

Further, Secretary Hickel told a Senate panel, the Government should beef up the United States Geological Survey so it can do independent geological work before private leases are granted for exploration and production.

Secretary Hickel, whose appointment, Secretary Hickel, whose appointment wha felt he was too closely tied to oil interests, was warmly received by the subcommittee members, who applauded his suggestions.

Survey Chief Backs Bid

He was backed up by Dr. William T. Pecora, director of the Geological Survey, who described his agency as being in the "unfortunate position" of depending on private companies for detailed geological information.

Dr. Pecora said, the Geological Survey is not able to provide factual information on the fair market value of areas leased, for example, to oil companies. Such information could lead to greater Federal revenues from the companies, he suggested.

Secretary Hickel appeared before the Senate Public Works Subcommittee on Air and Water Pollution to support a bill that would require oil companies and drillers to clean up accidental oil spills at their own expense and to provide other safety measures.

Good Chance of Passing

The measure, sponsored by Senator Edmund S. Muskie, Democrat of Maine, is given a good chance of passage by the end of the month. It would prohibit the Santa Barbara, Calif., area, or similar situation that might produce pollution. The bill is presently limited to oil. These substances might be detergents, acids, chemicals and other materials.

Dutch Approve Role For Married Priests

Special to The New York Times

THE HAGUE, Feb. 28 — The seven Roman Catholic bishops of the Netherlands have agreed to experiment with a new kind of married priests are allowed to preach.

This was announced last night by Msgr. Theo Zwartkruis, Bishop of Haarlem, who were among the other bishops on a conflict that had arisen between him and the parish at the University of Amsterdam.

Continued on Page 7, Column 3

world Communist movement, a prospect hardly likely to please the Soviet Union.

The statement of the Czechoslovak Communist party's democratic platform was contained in a long article devoted to the 50th anniversary of the founding of the Comintern, known as the Comintern. The instrument for directing the world Communist movement along policy lines set by Moscow, the Comintern, was dissolved in 1943.

Used for Purges

By contrasting the relative openness of the Comintern's early years under Lenin with its later use as a vehicle for purges by Stalin, the article indirectly criticized the present leaders of the Kremlin by implying parallels.

In what amounted to a condemnation of the Soviet occupation, a subject theoretically out of bounds for Czechoslovak politicians and journalists, Rude Pravo said:

"Lenin and some other Communist internationaries were aware that a permanently active concentration of revolutionary forces could not be fruitful through mere military occupation.

Varied Struggles Cited

"The variety of conditions in which Communists wage their struggle has developed to such an extent that principles of democratic centralism, corresponding to parties can no longer be applied to their mutual relations."

This meant that unquestioning obedience to the leadership of one party—the concept of democratic centralism—did not entail unquestioning obedience to the Kremlin as the leader of the world movement.

Rude Pravo warned that any "mechanical imitation" of Soviet-imposed policy "tends to violate ties of international solidarity rather than strengthen them."

"Permanent foundations of

Continued on Page 12, Column 1

announcements.

The first was a Soviet diplomatic note handed by Moscow's Ambassador here, Pyotr A. Abrasimov, to the East German Foreign Minister, Otto Winzer. The second was a "declaration" issued by the East German State Press Office.

Both indicated that East Germany, acting with Soviet approval, would apply selective restrictions on the movement of West Berlin industrial products and traffic on the roads and autobahns to West Germany.

Soviet Expert on Hand

West Berlin factories" were secretly producing a variety of weapons for West Germany's armed forces, the Soviet note said such "unlawful" shipments could effectively counter" this traffic.

Marshal Yakubovsky confirmed immediately after his arrival in Berlin with the East German Communist party lead er. Walter Ulbricht, on "important matters," according to A.D.N., the official East German news agency.

The Warsaw Pact command er—attended by the top Soviet expert on German affairs, Via-

A Shift of Power In Syria Is Reported

By DANA ADAMS SCHMIDT
Special to The New York Times

BEIRUT, Lebanon, Saturday, March 1 — The Syrian Army, under the Defense Minister, Lieut. Gen. Hafez al-Assad, has taken control of the Government of Syria in what appears to be an attempt to force military cooperation with Iraq against Israel on the eastern front.

General al-Assad and Maj. Gen. Mustafa Tlas, were reported today to have placed under house arrest three men, Maj. Gen. Salah Jadid, the leftist Baath party's strongman.

President al-Atassi unexpectedly did not appear Thursday at prayers in Damascus's principal mosque during the Id el

Continued on Page 11, Column 1

A Day in the Life of **The New York Times**

A Day in the

Ruth Adler

Life of The New York Times

J. B. LIPPINCOTT COMPANY

Philadelphia and New York

A NEW YORK TIMES BOOK

For my mother

Foreword

This is the hour-by-hour story of an ordinary day at *The New York Times*. The day was picked at random a week in advance. No one knew whether Friday, February 28, 1969, would produce startling news or simply the basic stories that are the backbone of every issue.

Once the day was selected, the entire staff of The Times was alerted. Memos were posted in every department and sent to every national and foreign bureau. In them I asked: "If anything offbeat, amusing, harrowing or whatever occurs— that might make a sentence or a paragraph—please send it to me." In addition, I asked a dozen or so staff members in New York and around the world to keep detailed logs of their activities throughout the chosen day. "I want not only what you do," I told them, "but, as far as possible, why you do it."

The response was marvelous.

Newspapermen write wonderful memos, for this gives them a chance to indulge the subjective eye and ear that they are unable to use in their profession of objective reporting. Their reports were crammed not only with descriptions of what they had seen and heard and done but also with accounts of what they felt and thought. Fascinating oddments abounded. The Times's publisher, Arthur Ochs Sulzberger, included in his memo, for example, this notation:

"9:36 to 9:37 A.M.: Threw out a dead tulip."

The book is focused on the daily news operation. To the thousands of men and women who work for The Times in hundreds of different capacities and who are not mentioned in these pages, my apologies and regrets. Without their contributions there could be no *New York Times*.

Many of the people who *are* mentioned have changed jobs at The Times since February 28, 1969. It would be a futile exercise to list all the changes here, for many will have moved again in the months that elapse between this writing and publication day. But the process of gathering and editing the news and putting out the paper remains unchanged—and that is what this book is all about.

Ruth Adler
New York City
May 1971

Contents

● ● ● ● ● ● ● ● ● ● *The Presses Roll*

A section of photographs will be found following page 118.

The World Watch

· · 3 a.m.

"Good night!"

The call comes from Tom Daffron, assistant news editor. It echoes through the almost deserted block-long newsroom in *The New York Times*'s plant on 43d Street west of Times Square. To the dozen editors, rewrite men, clerks and copyboys who have closed the final edition, it is the signal to go home. The paper has gone to bed.

It is one minute after three.

. . .

Half a world away, in South Vietnam, the unending, frustrating war grinds on. It is 4 o'clock on a blistering hot afternoon, and Times men are cadging rides by plane, helicopter and truck to see for themselves what is going on in the field and to gather material that will give their dispatches more depth and meaning than can be derived from the handouts at the official briefings.

Charles Mohr, a veteran Far East hand who is The Times's chief correspondent in Southeast Asia, is riding a jeep down a rutted road toward Saigon. He spent last night with an artillery unit that had been mercilessly pounded a few days earlier at the start of the Vietcong spring offensive. Mohr thought the unit a likely target for attack but guessed wrong. He was roused from sleep this morning by the voice of the battalion

3

commander saying: "Wake up. It's six A.M., and we're still alive." Now he is heading south to Saigon, having hitched a ride with two enlisted men. The jeep bounces along in the choking dust. One of the G.I.'s mans a swivel-mounted gun. On the front seat beside the other, who is driving, are boxes of ammunition, grenades and two M-16 rifles. Just in case.

Not far away, 6 miles north of Saigon, young Joseph B. Treaster, getting his baptism as a reporter in Vietnam, pulls into 1st Division headquarters. For three hours he and a colleague from Reuters, the British news agency, have charged around in their station wagon, up and down dirt trails and pot-holed macadam strips, searching for the craftily concealed command post of five companies engaged in a twenty-four-hour struggle with an estimated total of 100 North Vietnamese. In Saigon, earlier in the day, Treaster had learned about the fighting, so close to the edge of the city, and had been sure he would run across something worth reporting if only he could find out where the action was. But he, too, had guessed wrong. "It looks like it's about over now," an operations officer tells him. "There were pieces of bodies and blood all over the place. We estimated we killed about fifty." The roar of helicopters landing, carrying troops who had been battling in a nearby swamp, sends Treaster rushing out of divisional headquarters, notebook at the ready, to talk to the weary men.

Meanwhile, Terence Smith, the bureau chief—a cool, bespectacled young man who looks more like a choirmaster than a war correspondent—climbs the stairs to The Times's office on the second floor of 203 Tu-Do, the main street of Saigon. He has come from the daily briefing of correspondents, commonly called the Five O'Clock Follies because it once started at 5 in the afternoon, though now it begins earlier. The Follies are staged two blocks away in an auditorium in the Vietnam National Press Center. A statistical rundown of the fighting is given by "ground" and "air" briefers, but it is stylized and dull.

In the office, Smith begins to wade through the mounds of single-spaced official handouts that he picked up at the briefing. They describe, antiseptically, the military actions. Nobody dies—he's KIA (killed in action); nobody is wounded —he's WIA. Smith will wait, before he writes the daily military roundup, to see what realities Mohr and Treaster bring in from the field. First-edition deadline is still sixteen hours away.

• • •

In hot and steaming Karachi, 8,000 miles from the home office, it is 1:30 in the afternoon. Joseph Lelyveld sits in the luxurious residence of Zulfikar Ali Bhutto, West Pakistan's most vivid political figure, who is challenging Pakistan's faltering President, Mohammad Ayub Khan. The extraordinarily rich furnishings include Oriental rugs too handsome to be stepped on. "This is the only house I've ever been in," Lelyveld thinks to himself, "with Persian carpets on the ceiling."

• • •

In Nairobi, Kenya, it has rained for three nights. It is 11 o'clock on a sultry, heavily overcast morning, and lanky Lawrence Fellows is haggling with an Immigration officer over extension of the re-entry permit on his passport. He may have to go on short notice to any country in Black Africa, and the permit will let him go and come at will. Without it, he will have difficulty leaving Kenya and even more difficulty getting back in. The permit must be renewed each year, and in his four years in the country Fellows has never had trouble with it before. But the Immigration Department has been Africanized, and the English expatriate who formerly did the job in minutes has been replaced by a black citizen of Kenya— replaced, in fact, by seven or eight people. Efficiency seems to have suffered in the process.

• • •

As the hands of the newsroom clocks on 43d Street inch forward, Max Frankel and Robert B. Semple, Jr., board a bus at the Excelsior Hotel in Rome to begin a long day's travel to Paris, the last stop on President Nixon's eight-day tour of five European capitals. Both men wear thick glasses, but the resemblance ends there. Frankel is a semiportly whiz kid who, at thirty-nine, is chief of The Times's Washington bureau. Semple, a tall, gangly, buoyant Ivy Leaguer in his mid-twenties, covers the White House.

This morning, though, he is not so buoyant. He is sick. The medical corpsman who travels with the press has him plugged with green pills, red pills, blue pills. He has never before visited Rome, and now, at 9 A.M., as he leaves it, he cannot legitimately claim to have seen it on this trip.

The press bus pulls up in front of the Quirinale Palace, where Nixon bids farewell to the President of Italy. There is little substance but much cautious good cheer in the exchange of departure statements. More farewells at the Chigi Palace, this time with the Italian Premier, and more statements full of mutual expressions of good will.

There's no real meat to what Nixon and the Italian leaders say. And even if there were, Frankel and Semple realize, their remarks would rate only a few paragraphs toward the middle of the story that will be filed tonight from Paris. All through the trip Nixon and the press have been pointing toward de Gaulle; and even if de Gaulle says nothing, he will command the reporters' attention tonight.

. . .

In London, at 9 A.M., it is damp and cold, and The Times's bureau is empty save for John Rothera, the early man in the wire room. His first message of the day, from Pakistan, has just come in on one of the room's dozen or so printers. It says: TOPPING ARRIVED KARACHI LELYVELD. Rothera transmits it immediately over the leased cable that links the London bureau with The Times's newsroom in New York. The message is from Joe Lelyveld, whose huge beat encompasses India and Pakistan. He is away from his home base, New Delhi, and is informing Seymour Topping, the foreign news editor, of his whereabouts.

· · ·

Though most of the men and women who work for The Times in New York are asleep, Clive Barnes, the indefatigable drama and dance critic, is still at work. Earlier in the night he attended the opening of a Broadway play, hurried back to the office and in forty minutes typed out a review. (He did not like the play. Nor, it seemed, did anyone else; it closed after four performances.) Now, looking like a flabby Napoleon after a six-month campaign on which he had forgotten to take along a barber, Barnes sits in the kitchen of his Manhattan apartment drinking black coffee and dictating notes into a tape recorder for an article he is preparing for the Sunday "Magazine" on the dancers Erik Bruhn and Carla Fracci.

And Art Critic John Canaday, a victim of insomnia, gets to worrying, as insomniacs will, about the story he has written for tomorrow's paper on the artist Grandma Moses. He turns on a light in his Sutton Place apartment, rereads the carbon copy he brought home with him and decides it will do, after all. He checks his alarm clock, which is set for 6 A.M., and falls asleep.

· · ·

After Tom Daffron's "Good night" echoes through the news-room floor at 3:01 A.M., Bill Chambers, the late-shift make-up editor, dials the stereotype foreman in the pressroom. "Six back at three and good night," he says. The foreman gets the message. It means that six pages have been opened in the composing room for late news or corrections and, when the stereotypers have molded the six plates for the presses, they can shut up shop.

Dick Roberts, the late man on the metropolitan desk, dials the telephone operator who sits the overnight watch on the switchboard eight floors above the newsroom. "Good night," he says, her signal to call The Times's reporter at Manhattan Police Headquarters and inform him that the paper is closed —finished for the night. He can go home. No matter what news breaks now, it will not make today's paper.

The editors type brief notes to the heads of their respective day desks. Allan Siegal, who keeps the late watch on the foreign desk, taps out a memo that reads like hieroglyphics: "Viet—updating by Smith for 2d edn. (sub for AP folo). A few extra shorts sent up. Otherwise quiet." This means that nothing much happened after the day editors left for the night, that late details from Terence Smith in Saigon arrived in time to be substituted for details provided earlier by the Associated Press.

Reading these cryptic overnight messages will be the first order of business for the day editors when they reach their desks some six hours from now, a quick way to catch up with developments that occurred after the early editions were printed last night. The main news desks—foreign, national and metropolitan—are staffed sixteen or seventeen hours out of every twenty-four. The editors and their assistants on each desk work overlapping shifts beginning around 10 in the morning and continuing until "Good night."

· · ·

At 3:25, Siegal, the last staff man on the floor, shrugs into his overcoat. On the way out he stops by the wire room, adjacent to the newsroom, with a cable for Terence Smith. It says: LONDON TERRYSMITH YOUR WAR INSERTS INSIDED SECOND EDITION ALLBEST. The message isn't going to surprise Smith. Communications from Saigon are spotty, and sometimes his copy is delayed or garbled in transmission. By telling him that his story landed inside the paper in the second edition, Siegal gives him a chance to judge how much detail he needs to repeat in his next day's story.

Twenty minutes after Siegal hands the cable to the wire-room clerk, it is in Smith's hands in Saigon as he awaits the return of Mohr and Treaster from the field.

· · ·

By 3:30, the dimmed and deserted newsroom on the third floor of the fourteen-story plant is quiet save for the chattering of wire-room machines as stories continue to come in from the earth's far corners. Two overnight clerks strip the copy from the machines and pile it in baskets to be distributed at 8 A.M. to the news desks that will handle it.

One floor above the newsroom, in the composing room, 200 printers on the lobster—or overnight—shift turn to stripping the paper—breaking up the type and throwing the metal into hellboxes, receptacles for used type. Later, the metal will be gathered up, melted down and used another day. In the sub-basement the thundering presses pound out the final copies of the run, and at street level mailers and deliverers direct the flow of freshly printed papers to waiting trucks.

Siegal rides the elevator to the lobby, nods good night to the plant patrolman on duty and passes through the revolving doors to the street. It has been a quiet night. It won't take him long to unwind as it does some nights when he tries not to think about what might have been: how they could have telephoned faster to a correspondent and closed an edition ten minutes earlier, or gotten a more comprehensive story into some copies of the paper. Tonight, as he walks toward Broadway to hail a cab, he is relaxed.

Forty-third Street is pretty seedy at 3:30 in the morning, grimy and littered with bits and pieces of *The New York Times,* clogged with delivery trucks, motors running, awaiting their final loads of papers. Half a dozen drunks sleep it off in the mausoleumlike doorways cut into the brick buildings across the street from The Times. The gray sandstone plant, which stands in the middle of the block west of Times Square, is black against the night sky. Except for the fourth-floor composing room, all fourteen floors above the street are dark or almost dark. Charwomen and porters push their brooms and mops around the deserted floors, which will come to life again when the nine-to-fivers—business office and advertising crews —stream through the white marble lobby to the elevators.

· · 4 a.m.

The world watch shifts to London, where it is 10 A.M. The foreign desk in New York will not be staffed for another six hours, and if an earth-shaking story breaks now, Anthony Lewis, the London bureau chief, or one of his staff, will telephone Topping at his home in Scarsdale. If emergency moves are called for, Topping will dictate any messages necessary to start correspondents toward the scene of action. Being roused from deep sleep is an occupational hazard of the foreign news editor, and Topping has learned to come instantly alert no matter what hour the telephone rings. And what's more, he always remembers to say thank you.

The London bureau, largest of The Times's foreign outposts, occupies the fifth floor of *The Times* of London building on Printing House Square. It is the communications way station, the major relay point between the home office on 43d Street and correspondents throughout the world. On an average day, 30,000 words hurtle through its wire room on the way to New York over two leased cables that carry copy instantaneously across the Atlantic. A spur of these cables links the London and Paris bureaus, and a third circuit—partly radio and, therefore, susceptible to weather conditions that can knock it out or garble the copy—provides instantaneous communication between New York, London, and Vietnam and other parts of the Far East.

London is more centrally located than New York to most world capitals, and it is easier to make contact from there. This is important, particularly in time of crisis when a country's communications facilities tend to be the first thing to falter. The London bureau is frequently able to get through to correspondents—in Athens during the generals' coup, in Czechoslovakia during the Russian occupation, for example —when it is impossible to make contact from New York without, at best, interminable delays.

It is also practical and economical for The Times to use the London bureau as a relay station rather than rely on direct communication between the editors in New York and correspondents abroad. There is no restriction on the number of words that can be transmitted back and forth between New York and London over the leased wires, whereas if messages and copy are sent direct, even at press rates, the costs are astronomical.

But the bureau is far more than simply a routine way station. The copy that pours in to London is sorted, assembled, read and, if garbled in transmission, straightened out before it is passed on to New York. Because of the time difference, this is a boon to the editors in the home office. By the time they show up at their desks in the morning, copy that might have been incomprehensible when it reached London several hours earlier lies before them, organized and in sequence.

Copy arrives in the London bureau wire room in several ways. Some of it is dictated by correspondents into telephone recorders, and transcribed by bureau hands and forwarded to New York. Some arrives on teletype and telex machines. Teletype copy, which travels over regular telegraph and cable lines, must be repunched by bureau operators for transmission to 43d Street—typed out, that is, on sending machines. Telex copy comes in on tape, with a print-out. The tape goes through to New York without repunching, but the bureau checks the raw copy on the print-out for transmission errors.

At 10:20 in the morning, Anthony Lewis emerges from his home in Islington, a rather slummy part of London now partly restored. He steps into the waiting chauffeur-driven office Jaguar for the ten-minute drive to Printing House Square. In the spacious bureau newsroom he pauses at the five-man news desk now occupied only by Harry Vosser, the day editor. Vosser is reading through a duplicate of cable copy from Philip Shabecoff in Tokyo that has gone through London to New York. He wants to make sure it did not get garbled in transmission. If it did, he will ask the cable office in Tokyo for clarification.

Lewis sits down at his desk in the bureau chief's office, which looks out on the dome of St. Paul's Cathedral and gives, in the distance, a glimpse of the Thames. He glances at the "fronting" cable sent out from New York the night before to inform correspondents around the world how their stories fared in today's paper. He is pleased to see that John Lee's story on the raising of British bank rates made page 1. Lee is the bureau's economics expert. Lewis reads through the cable copy of Max Frankel's story sent from Rome last night. The story, appraising President Nixon's visit to the Italian capital, is in today's *New York Times,* but it will be tomorrow, at the earliest, before the paper, shipped air freight from New York, reaches London. If a bureau is not on a direct air route from New York, it can be several days, sometimes a week or more, before the paper arrives. The "fronting" provides the correspondent with his only immediate word as to whether his story has made the front page or an inside page, has been drastically cut for space, or has been held over.

While Lewis goes through his mail and sips a cup of office-brewed tea, there's a flurry of activity in a cubicle to one side of the newsroom. Heather Bradley, the London representative of the Sunday department of The Times, is dictating to her secretary a spate of memos for the New York editors of the special Sunday sections: to Harvey Shapiro, articles editor of the Sunday "Magazine," suggestions for pieces on Syria and Turkey and the names of British writers who might do them; to the Sunday travel editor, a suggestion for a piece on the 150th anniversary of the Burlington Arcade; to Seymour Peck, editor of the "Arts and Leisure" section, a suggestion for an interview with Pierre Boulez, who is about to take over as BBC Symphony Orchestra conductor. Miss Bradley's secretary has already clipped cartoons from ten London morning papers for Robert Clurman, editor of "The Week in Review" section. All this material will go to the Sunday department in New York in an air-freight packet that will be picked up at noon.

Not all the news in The Times is produced by the daily news staff. A separate Sunday department, under the direction of Sunday Editor Daniel Schwarz, concerns itself with the "Magazine," "Book Review," "Week in Review," "Arts and Leisure," and "Travel and Resorts" sections of the Sunday paper. Among its ninety men and women are full-time representatives in London, Paris and Washington who recommend articles from their respective listening posts, suggest possible writers—sometimes staff men, sometimes freelancers—and follow up on assignments.

• • •

In West Berlin, David Binder and Ralph Blumenthal, The Times's correspondents in Germany, have slept off the exhaustion of two days of Nixon coverage and are strolling, in suddenly springlike weather, along the Kurfürstendamm, the city's most elegant thoroughfare. Both men came from Bonn, their permanent post, for the Nixon visit, and Binder will stay on to cover the upcoming West German elections.

Their talk turns to the percolating crisis building up around them—the possibility of Communist reprisals because of West Germany's insistence on holding the elections in Berlin. Binder, the senior man, gained some insight into Communist thinking while he was covering Eastern Europe before he was assigned to Germany three years ago. He holds to the opinion that the present threats are more a temporary harassment than the prelude to a major East-West crisis.

. . .

In Moscow, it is bright and clear and very cold, and Henry Kamm is about ready to go home to lunch. Before he climbs the six floors to his apartment, he asks Boris Zakharou, his interpreter, to come into his office. The bureau chief's office is the smallest room in a three-room flat on the second floor of 12/24 Sadova Samotechnaya, a massive tan building, a ghetto of sorts, in which foreign diplomats and journalists in the Soviet Union not only work but, in most cases, live.

Kamm has been mulling over a piece in yesterday's *Pravda,* the official Communist party newspaper, that deals with a constant problem in the Soviet Union—the scarcity of cultural and entertainment facilities in small towns. The article took the form of a letter from fifty young people in a Ukrainian town, who were sharply critical of the lady director of the local House of Culture. Kamm would like to do something with the story—but what and how? He asks Boris to put in a phone call to the lady criticized in *Pravda.* He probably won't reach her, he figures; the town is small and he has no telephone number—and, anyhow, why should a lady just attacked in the Soviet press take a chance of talking with *The New York Times?* But why not try?

. . .

In Jerusalem, at eleven in the morning, James Feron has already covered a major story—the state funeral of Premier Levi Eshkol. Feron has been up since dawn. He rode the press bus to the first part of the ceremony at the Knesset (Parliament) Building, then returned to the Public Information Office in Jerusalem to watch on television the second half of the service, the burial at Mount Herzl. Newsmen had been given a choice: attend one service or the other or watch both on TV, strict security precautions making it impossible for them to at-

tend both. Feron chose to go to the Knesset. He stood for an
hour on the cold, wet grass not yet dried by the day's warm
sun before the service started at 8 A.M.

Since he knew he would be watching the burial on TV, he
had gone to Mount Herzl the previous day to fix the scene in
his mind. He made a note to put high up in his story the
touching fact that Eshkol would be buried in a grave next to
Yosef Sprinzak, the man who had talked him into coming to
Palestine five decades ago.

Now, in the Public Information Office newsroom, journalists fill each other in and swap observations on details of the
ceremony they have witnessed. Feron picks up some detail
that duplicates what he already knows, but he gets some that
is fresh—a description, for example, of the huge crowds along
the route from the Knesset to Mount Herzl. He also picks up a
tip that he will pursue later in the day: Yigal Allon, the acting
Premier, is going to receive the visiting American delegation,
headed by Robert H. Finch, Secretary of Health, Education
and Welfare, at his office at 3 P.M. Feron will be there. The
meeting will no doubt be off bounds to reporters, but he'll try
to put some questions to the Americans as they enter or leave.

He's called to the phone. His wife tells him that a cable has
just come from the picture desk in New York asking which of
two photographers assigned by them to cover the funeral
should get the credit line under the pictures. He'll check it
out.

• • •

Back in the Immigration Office in Nairobi, where he's still
bucking red tape in his effort to get his re-entry permit, Larry
Fellows impatiently wonders if he is going to get any lunch or,
in fact, get anything at all done this day. He had planned to
drive to Kajiado to see an Indian trader he had known for a
couple of years and find out if he had managed to escape the
purge of Indian traders. The Kenya government had said it
was getting rid of 3,000 noncitizen traders. Ali, the trader in

Kajiado, would make a good story whether he had been purged or merely lived in fear of being purged. If it had not been for him, there would be no place called Kajiado. He set up his store in the middle of the Masai plain, and a ramshackle little town grew up around him. He sells everything that is sold there and doubles as postmaster, letter-writer for the illiterates, and unofficial Mayor.

Fellows decides to leave his passport until tomorrow in the hope that the officials will get to work on it. Outdoors it is raining again, so he dogtrots the few blocks to the *East African Standard* in the center of town, where he shares an office with several other correspondents. He presses the elevator button but doesn't wait to be assured that the old contraption is still not working. He wants to make a telephone call before offices empty for lunch, so he walks up to the third floor.

He can't get a line at first; then he gets a busy signal. Telephoning in Nairobi is frustrating and time-consuming; the lines are perpetually overloaded. He finally gets through to a lawyer who represents an editor charged with sedition by the Uganda government who was acquitted, but is still in jail. Fellows is calling on the off-chance that the editor might have been released. He hasn't been—so no story there. He flips through the copy that has come in on the local news ticker. Nothing of interest. He'll drive to Kajiado after a quick lunch.

• • •

In Paris, Henry Tanner, the Swiss-born bureau chief, is in the office at 37 rue Caumartin at the unusually early, for him, hour of 10. Before the Nixon entourage, bearing Frankel and Semple, arrives in early afternoon, he must write a 1,000-word piece for Sunday's "Week in Review" section, a piece already twelve hours overdue. Natasha Chassagne, the bureau secretary, is startled to see Tanner at his desk when she arrives a few minutes behind him. The bureau chauffeur awaits his assignments, and a second chauffeur, hired to drive Frankel and Semple during the week end, has already reported for duty.

Tanner flips through the British and German newspapers. He is seeking enlightenment for his "Review" piece, which is supposed to sum up and evaluate the Nixon trip from the European point of view. Also, there's the incontestable truth that as long as he reads, he doesn't have to start writing.

But at 10:40 he can delay no longer. He locks the door to his office, tells Mme. Chassagne he wants no phone calls, and starts to type. At that moment, 3,500 miles away, the last delivery trucks are pulling out of the 43d Street loading sheds, headlights ablaze, carrying their cargoes of final editions of this morning's *New York Times* to near and distant points.

· 5 a.m.

Dusk has settled over Vietnam, and Charlie Mohr has reached Gia Dinh, a Saigon suburb, on the armed jeep that is carrying him back from the field. That's the end of the road for the G.I.'s, so Mohr hails a cyclo, or motorcycle taxi, for the ride into town. He fits his tall, muscular frame into the passenger gondola hooked to the front of the machine, leans back and reflects that in Vietnam one of a reporter's most exhausting and time-consuming jobs is simply getting himself to the scene of a story and back.

It's a few minutes before 7 P.M. when the cyclo drops him at The Times's bureau in downtown Saigon. Mohr climbs the stairs to the long, rectangular room that is the office. He walks gingerly, trying to dodge the cockroaches that skitter across the tile floor. He half-heartedly swats at a gecko on the wall, but misses. These lizards, which scuttle up the walls and across the ceilings, are useful; they eat the mosquitoes. He takes a cold beer, which tastes good, from the refrigerator.

For a few minutes he talks with Terry Smith, who is organizing his notes and checking out by telephone the official report of the forty-five different shellings that occurred around the country during the last twenty-four hours. Then Mohr takes off for the Continental, his hotel across the street, to wash off the layers of dust and change from jungle fatigues into sport shirt and slacks. He looks forward to a leisurely dinner before he returns to the office to write about his experiences last night at 25th Division base headquarters. He knows that the foreign desk in New York likes to have routine cable copy such as this in its hands by 12 noon—seven hours from now—to clear its decks for late-breaking spot news.

Joe Treaster pulls into the bureau a few minutes behind Mohr. He and Smith go over the notes from his interviews with the soldiers who battled in the suburban swamps. Smith decides to wrap Treaster's story into his own war lead. Treaster hides his disappointment. It is the bureau chief's prerogative to use whatever material he feels will enhance the daily war lead, and Treaster knows that his eyewitness details will flesh out and give dimension to what might otherwise be a flat and statistical account of the day's fighting.

Treaster stops by the Reuters office down the hall to pick up the colleague with whom he shared the drive this afternoon to 1st Division headquarters. They drive to Treaster's apartment, where he whips up a dinner of charcoal-broiled beef and *kimchi* (pickled vegetables).

        • • •

In the Middle East the noonday sun is hot. Jim Feron is at his home in Jerusalem, typing up his notes on the Eshkol funeral. Home is a spacious nine-room Arab house, one room of which is his office. When the family noise gets unbearable, he can close himself off.

Working for The Times abroad had seemed romantic to Feron, but not much more than that, when he came on the paper as a night copyboy in 1952. He was twenty-four, out of college, Army service behind him. His primary goal was to get on the local news staff. Being a foreign correspondent seemed so far beyond a copyboy's wildest dreams that he seldom thought about it.

Feron had been an average, straight C, student through high school and Marietta College in Ohio. He wasn't terribly interested in anything so far as career was concerned until, in his senior year, he worked on his college newspaper. Suddenly he thought journalism was for him.

As he hauled copy around the newsroom floor at night, he realized that all the copyboys were in the same boat—none of them got a chance to show what they could really do. The Times was too big to act as a training school for young reporters. So Feron enrolled at the graduate School of Journalism at Columbia and sandwiched in classes between pay-job hours. He was graduated at the top of his class. The Times's metropolitan editor was impressed with his record and offered him a job writing copy instead of carrying it. He worked up the journalistic ladder—police reporter in Queens, general assignment, night rewrite, then a stint at the United Nations bureau on the East River. Five years passed before the newsroom's personnel chief asked him if he would be interested in going overseas. The answer was emphatically yes.

Foreign correspondents have always been the glamour boys of journalism. They get around. They catch glimpses of the world's great and near-great. They have front seats at the big shows that make history—wars, revolutions, the great spectacles. Young reporters have always leaped at the opportunity to become a foreign correspondent.

But the number of reporters who say they want to go overseas tends to decline as they move ahead. Some find a local area of news they would like to cover; some assume responsibilities, such as a family, that they think will make it too difficult to work abroad. At the same time, the list of persons The Times wants to send overseas declines, or is narrowed down, as young reporters fail to develop in the way they had been expected to. Nowadays, too, there are real issues to be resolved right at home, issues that grip young men and women in a way that did not exist, say, ten years ago.

Some reporters like to try a foreign assignment just for the experience. Jim Feron, for example, did not sell his house on

Long Island when he and his wife and two small sons first went overseas to London in 1961. Feron and his wife looked upon the assignment as an experiment that might be brief. Once abroad, and liking it, they decided to keep the house anyhow, as a sort of anchor, a place they could tell the kids was "home."

They soon discovered, though, that home is where they are. Now they move from post to post with their furniture and their possessions, and home becomes wherever they put them and settle as a family, which now includes four small Ferons.

Some reporters have their eye on an overseas assignment from the very start of their careers and want it with much greater intensity than Feron experienced. Some are seen to have special qualifications and are approached by their superiors, though this has not always proved successful. Language is a good example. Reporters have been sent abroad with tremendous language qualifications but, once on the job, have revealed serious deficiencies, such as inability to "see" a story because they are too close to it.

Once abroad, a foreign correspondent must adjust to a whole new framework. He may find that he dislikes the essentially solitary nature of the work. Or he may discover that he cannot initiate stories, that he is unable to function independently, and seems always out of step with the home office.

On the other hand, some reporters become so adjusted to life abroad that they lose their perspective as to what should be regarded as news. To guard against this danger of overfamiliarity, The Times shifts its correspondents frequently, limiting a man's tour of duty in any one country. The theory is that a good reporter can cover Beirut as well as Bangkok.

Some families flourish abroad; others wilt. The role of the correspondent's wife cannot be ignored. Some are whiners; others are silent sufferers. But the wife who can accept the plusses and minuses and enjoy living abroad can make her husband's job that much more pleasant.

There are those who feel that working abroad is a bache-

lor's job. Edwin L. James, a former managing editor of The
Times, used to say when he was looking for a man to assign
overseas: "Find me a eunuch." He was fed up with complaints
from wives, one of whom threatened to sue The Times for
alienation of her husband's affections.

But many correspondents believe that a family can absorb
much more of the life of a country than a single man does and
that they thus contribute more to his reporting. There are
posts—Saigon, perhaps a few others—where a family would
be isolated, or even endangered. But a bachelor in New Delhi,
for example, has a much drearier life than does his married
counterpart.

The best part of working abroad, most correspondents
agree, is the freedom. A reporter who has the confidence of
his editor at home frequently makes his own assignments,
travels as he will, writes what he wants when he wants to. He
can orchestrate his output, inserting this or that feature when
and where he thinks it will be the most effective, varying his
report to give it color and zest and interest. He is, in other
words, pretty much his own boss. Of course, he works in close
coordination with his editor in the home office, but a really
good correspondent initiates most of his work. It's simply too
much for the foreign editor to sit at his desk on 43d Street
and say, for example: "What shall I have Feron do today?" For
the most part, Feron is finishing his day when the editor begins his.

It is a common misconception that foreign correspondents
lead dangerous, or at least thrilling, lives (except, of course,
those who are trapped in a shooting war). Interesting, even
challenging, is more like it. There are fewer certainties for the
man working abroad, but less of a routine. Endless hours are
devoted to the garbage details of life—government bureau-
cracies, just getting from one place to another. Frequently, it
is a piece of drudgery to go from A to B, often requiring the
most elegant side steps, slides and leaps.

Then there is the matter of getting the copy out. Half a correspondent's time can be spent simply accomplishing what the local reporter never thinks about—sending copy to the office. It requires knowledge of communications, bribery, patience, cajolery, threats. In some places, getting to the story and then sending it out occupy up to 90 per cent of a correspondent's time. The other 10 per cent, the easiest part, is spent covering the story and writing it.

In some ways, working overseas is like working at home —a bit easier here, a bit harder there. The pay is generally better—at least, the dollar goes a lot farther—and the hours longer. The assignments are more nebulous, but often the stories are vastly more interesting.

Yet foreign correspondents frequently elect to chuck it all and come home for local or national assignments. Their reasons vary: the kids' education, simple weariness, health, family responsibilities. Nowadays many correspondents feel that, as professional newsmen, they want to be part of the big story unfolding in the U.S.A.

The Ferons may one day feel this way. For the present, though, the independence of working overseas and the broadening experience, for their children as well as themselves, outweigh the occasional dangers and perpetual inconveniences.

Inconveniences, such as the muffled boom that shakes the windows of his Arab villa in Jerusalem as Jim types his notes on the funeral of Premier Levi Eshkol.

His wife, Jeanne, calls from the kitchen: "I know, you didn't hear a thing." A family joke. Jerusalem shakes under explosions several times a day. Some are terrorist bombings; others are construction demolitions or sonic booms. There's no telling which is which, and Feron has trained himself not to notice any of them. He knows if it is a terrorist bomb, one of his photographer friends will call to tell him. Photographers in Jerusalem stay close to the police. They tell the reporters partly through friendship and partly because they know there will be no demand for their pictures unless the reporters file stories on the bombings. But today's boom is nothing—at least it's not a terrorist bomb.

Feron turns on the radio and attaches his tape recorder to catch the midday news broadcast. The Israeli radio has two English-language broadcasts a day, and they frequently yield story ideas that can be stored away on tape and taken off at leisure. Today, the half-hour description of the Eshkol funeral contains many specific details about the burial at Mount Herzl that Feron had missed on television.

The phone breaks into the broadcast. The duty officer at the Public Information Office is calling with an Army announcement that Egyptian snipers opened fire three times during the morning along the Suez Canal. Feron will be tied up with the funeral story most of the day, so he calls Moshe Brilliant in Tel Aviv to ask him to write the military roundup. Brilliant, a Brooklyn-born Israeli, is The Times's resident correspondent in Israel. Wise and knowledgeable about the country, he has served for two decades as an indispensable aid to rotating bureau chiefs.

He will write the military story, he tells Feron. He knows about the snipers. He gets the full range of official announcements from the Army press office in Tel Aviv.

• • •

One hundred and fifty miles to the north—but a world away as accessibility goes in the Israeli-Arab scheme—Dana Adams Schmidt is at lunch at an Arab waterfront restaurant in Beirut. He has as his guest James P. Brown, the Middle East expert of The Times's editorial board. Mr. Brown is passing through Lebanon on the first leg of a tour that will take him to all the Arab countries and, finally, to Israel to gather background material for his editorial writing.

They are dining with two Lebanese: Schmidt's assistant, Ihsan Hijazi, an amiable and knowledgeable man with the memory of an elephant; and Ghassan Kanafani, an editorial writer for a leftist Lebanese newspaper. Kanafani is one of the few Arabs who esteem *The New York Times* as the newspaper that prints both sides of the question, including the Arab side. This is high praise, for he is also the spokesman for the radical Popular Front for the Liberation of Palestine. Kanafani was delighted to accept Schmidt's luncheon invitation, but he resisted the suggestion that they meet at the popular St. Georges Hotel. Americans are not too popular in Lebanon, and Schmidt got the impression that Kanafani preferred not to be seen dining with Americans in such a public place as the St. Georges.

Schmidt has had an interesting but unsensational morning. No matter what the rest of the day brings it will not surprise him, for he knows that a correspondent's life in this Mideast listening post is a series of normal days capped by wacky, unpredictable, slam-bang climaxes.

He arose at 7 to drive his son to the American Community School. Back home, which is also his office, he read the English- and French-language newspapers and decided that Lebanese shenanigans were not likely to interest The Times's foreign news desk in New York.

He's well aware that The Times's interest in Lebanon lies not in its own incredibly complex politics but in its role as a relatively neutral, relatively free and relatively safe platform from which to observe the rest of the Middle East.

The papers are full of stories about the exploits of Al Fatah, the Palestinian guerrilla organization. Schmidt puts in a call to The Times's stringer in Amman, Suleiman Abdullah Schleiffer, a Jew converted to Islam and a first-rate reporter, hoping to propose that Schleiffer prepare a roundup of guerrilla claims. But the telephone lines are down. They often are, inexplicably.

Mohamed, The Times's English-speaking driver-interpreter, arrives at the Schmidt home in midmorning with a receipt from Pan American air freight. He has just sent off a story about Al Fatah and the commandos that Schmidt, on a recent expedition to Jordan, had written and taken pictures to illustrate. The packet will be in New York tonight, a vast improvement over the mails, which often take eight to ten days.

Schmidt's wife, Tania, departs with Mohamed to do some shopping. As Tania spends, she also collects—impressions. She'll bring back a report on what the housewives and merchants are complaining about, the mood of the town, chitchat that enhances her husband's understanding of the country and its people.

The rest of Schmidt's morning is taken up with routine. He studies Hijazi's review of the local press, which includes a report on the growing tension between the Army and the Baath party in neighboring Syria. He tries, still without success, to complete that call to Amman. He reads the mail and cables that Mohamed has brought from the Hotel St. Georges. Schmidt uses the hotel address because the chances of getting delivery are better there than at home. And the hotel concierge, an obliging fellow, telephones all over town to announce the arrival of a cable, read it over the phone and collect the answer.

Now, at lunch, the talk is lively. Jim Brown is getting the education he came for. He's intrigued to learn that Kanafani, unlike most Arab journalists, believes it is important to "know your enemy." He reads Hebrew, studies the Israeli press, knows Israeli politics. They talk about what will follow the death of Eshkol. They introduce Brown to the pleasures of the *mezeh,* a table covered with several dozen little dishes of different kinds of vegetables, meats, fish, yoghurts and cheeses, fruits and delicacies—all washed down with beer or arak. They warn Brown about arak. It tastes like licorice but is not recommended for anyone who hopes to work that afternoon.

·· 6 a.m.

In the giant Pan Am jet carrying the Nixon press party from Rome to Paris, Bob Semple thinks wistfully of his Washington colleagues, still abed. It is high noon as the plane flies over the Alps, but it is only 6 A.M. in Washington. Semple motions to the stewardess for a martini. Frankel sticks with mineral water, though it's Semple, not Frankel, whose stomach is quivering. Lunch is served—steak or lobster. They go for steak, order it rare and receive it well done.

At 12:30 P.M., the jet begins its slow descent into Orly Airport. Semple hauls from his brief case a packet of background material prepared for him by the bureau librarian before he left Washington. The pace of the trip has been too fast to consult the material as often as he would have liked, but the issues all along have been clear enough. In Brussels, the story was NATO; in London, the feud between Britain and France over France's refusal to permit Britain's entry into the Common Market; in Bonn, the reassurances required by Chancellor Kiesinger that West Germany would not be threatened by proposed Soviet-American arms talks. But what will France be? Everything? Or nothing? The story could be simply summarized: "Richard M. Nixon arrived in Paris this afternoon to confer at length with Gen. de Gaulle, hoping thereby to put to rest the general's historic fears of American interference in

European affairs and enlist his support in a variety of common causes." Or something half that length.

But by tonight, Semple knows, someone—Frankel has not yet assigned the story—will have to come up with something to follow this. Or, he thinks hopefully, de Gaulle and Nixon just might provide some hard news. Nothing to do now but wait and see—and hope.

In the Paris bureau on rue Caumartin, the staff girds itself for the strenuous afternoon and night ahead. John Hess grumbles as he reads a cable that has come in overnight from Gerald Gold, assistant foreign news editor in New York. Hess, the bureau's Francophile and its connoisseur of food and wines, had filed a sentimental piece a few days earlier about the closing of the historic Paris food market, Les Halles, and its move to the suburbs. The piece, with pictures, is to run in tomorrow's paper as a feature at the top of the split page, the first page of the second section. The foreign copydesk, readying it for publication, has combed it for unanswered questions, and Gold's cable raises several points that the desk thinks need further explanation. Hess dashes off a testy reply:

REPLYING YOUR QUESTIONS: FIGURES ON HOW MANY TRUCKS ARE INVOLVED ARE PROBABLY FAKE, LIKE THE DAILY VIETNAM BODY COUNT. CALL IT A "VAST FLEET" IF YOU PREFER. LES HALLES, LAST EXPANDED IN 1850s TO SERVE 1.5 MILLION, NOW SERVES METROPOLITAN AREA OF 10 MILLION BUT ALSO, ON THE ONE HAND, ALL FRANCE TO SOME EXTENT, WHILE ON THE OTHER HAND, MUCH OF THE TRADE NOW BYPASSES MARKET, SO IT'S ANOTHER FAKE TO PUT A NUMBER TO ITS CUSTOMERS. MARKET IS SUPPOSED TO HANDLE 5,000 TONS OF FOOD A DAY, IF YOU LIKE. LET'S SEE, THAT'S METRIC TONS, WHICH MAKES HOW MANY OUNCES AVOIRDUPOIS?

Hess feels better after he has let off steam in the cable. He takes an anonymous phone call advising him that anti-Nixon youths have been breaking windows in the neighborhood and that the cops have put a number of persons under preventive arrest for the Nixon visit.

Tanner, who has finished half of his "Week in Review" piece, emerges from his office, and he and Hess hold the first of the day's many story conferences. They decide that Hess will keep an eye on possible anti-Nixon demonstrations. This, and other material related to the Nixon visit, will be worked up so that it can be turned into sidebars—separate stories alongside the main story—or else incorporated into the main story. When Frankel arrives—he is in charge of the Nixon story as it moves from one country to another—they will have another conference to decide who will cover what aspect of the trip tonight.

Tanner makes a flurry of phone calls to the American Embassy and to some of his American and French contacts. A bulletin has come in saying that Nixon will receive twenty private French citizens during his visit, and Tanner wants to find out who they are. He hopes to connect with one or two who feel friendly enough toward The Times to be willing to give him a full account of Nixon's remarks. But he gets no place; either no one knows who the citizens are, or no one's talking.

• • •

Across the English Channel, in the London bureau, one of the wire-room printers, on which copy and messages to New York are punched, chokes and jams. Rothera, the wire-room operator, sends for a mechanic. Lucky, he muses, that the breakdown came at 11 in the morning, one of the quietest hours of all the twenty-four, when New York is dark and silent.

It occurs to Anthony Lewis that it might be a good idea to have Gloria Emerson, the bureau's distaff reporter, look in on the House of Commons, which on Fridays considers private, nongovernment bills, and today might reach one of some interest—a modification of Sunday blue laws against paid sports and theaters. He calls the House of Commons whip's office; the bill will come up today. He tries to reach Gloria at home. No answer.

Alvin Shuster, one of the bureau's five reporters, wanders into Lewis's office to talk briefly about a story he's been working on: the threat of new regulations over British gambling casinos. The news peg, they agree, is the deadline this week end for new casino licenses. Shuster will finish the story today and file it tonight.

Gloria, a tall, dashing brunette, bounds into the bureau. She has been at Harrod's Department Store to open a charge account and to look at the store's boutique, the "way in" place for new trends in London fashions. No new trends, but a story idea came to her as she filled out her credit application. The clerk pointed to a line on the form asking for business or profession and said, "I wouldn't bother to fill that in. It's none of our business really." Why not check into the ease of opening a London charge account? She will.

But now she must rush to the House of Commons, where the office telephonist has booked her a seat. Unlike press galleries any place else in the world, no one can enter the Houses of Parliament galleries without first reserving a seat. An attendant stops Gloria and informs her she cannot go in until she removes her head scarf. Why, she asks, since ladies wear hats? No response. She removes her scarf.

Lewis spends the rest of the morning signing checks, looking over office bills, dictating letters. The London bureau is heavily manned, and administrative detail occupies a lot of the bureau chief's time. Its reporters, copy editors, wire-room operators, accountants, secretaries and receptionists add up to twenty-seven, and the bureau chief is responsible to New York for the whole operation.

• • •

As the first glimmer of light breaks over The Times's 43d Street plant, Larry Fellows turns his car off the main road out of Nairobi and heads south toward Kajiado. The forty-mile drive is over a road of murram—soft volcanic rock—and includes stretches that don't hold up in wet weather. Though the rain has stopped for the moment, the sky is leaden, the air oppressive. At the bank of the Athi River, Fellows decides to wait, before crossing the bridge, to see if any traffic comes the other way. It's the only sure sign that the road beyond the river is passable.

He has with him a few issues of *The New York Times* and a couple of magazines so he can catch up on his back reading while he waits. But he has developed a slight headache, and he wonders if this may not be a sign that the monsoon is shifting, that the Long Rains have really set in. The wind is from the southeast, another sign. But the Long Rains aren't due for another month. He'll have to wait and see.

· · ·

As the sound of the cuckoo—another harbinger of rain—breaks the African stillness, far away in New York the shrill ring of the alarm clock rouses A. M. Rosenthal, The Times's associate managing editor, from deep sleep in his Central Park West apartment. It's 7 o'clock, and he has a busy few hours before he takes the subway to 43d Street. He must get through The Times as well as other New York and Washington morning papers. As he reads, he will dictate a stream of notes and comments into a recorder—reminders to himself, memos to his newsroom colleagues, criticism of some stories, praise for others, ideas for the future. Daylight washes over Central Park as he pulls himself awake.

· 7 a.m.

James Reston is an early riser by instinct rather than by alarm clock. At 7 in the morning he is well into The Times over breakfast coffee in his apartment overlooking the East River. He reads not only with an eye for what is good and what could be better, but also for ideas for his three-times-a-week editorial page column on national affairs. Reston is a towering figure in journalism—the nation's leading pundit as well as the top news executive of The Times. As executive editor he is responsible to the publisher for the content of both the daily and Sunday papers. He concerns himself primarily with long-range plans and policy and with researching and writing his columns. Administration of the news staff is in the hands of Managing Editor Clifton Daniel; responsibility for putting together the daily paper falls to Associate Managing Editor A. M. Rosenthal.*

      • • •

All over New York and its suburbs, editors are doing their homework over morning coffee—reading The Times, reading

* A few months later Reston relinquished the title of executive editor, and with it his newsroom duties, to become a vice president of The Times and concentrate on his columns. At the same time Daniel also left the newsroom to become an associate editor, and Rosenthal was named managing editor.

the competition, appraising, comparing. They know that once they reach the newsroom, the race toward tomorrow's paper will leave them no time to scrutinize today's.

Andrew Ragona unlatches the front door of his home in Valley Stream, Long Island, and picks his *New York Times* off the stoop. He, though, barely glances at the front page. He turns quickly to page 2 and thumbs through the paper, examining each page with trained and critical eye, looking only at the ads—not so much for what they say as for how they shape up visually. In his job as director of advertising production, he is responsible for every display ad in The Times from the moment it enters the office until it is fitted into a page form in the composing room. (Display ads, with or without illustrations and using varying type sizes and design, constitute all advertising except classified—the small-type, single-column notices printed in the classified advertising columns.)

In his morning run-through, Ragona makes sure that illustrations are sharp and clear; that type and lettering are clean and crisp; that each ad on the whole looks pretty much as the advertiser expected. Occasionally, his caterpillar eyebrows jump. Despite sharpest watch, errors will sometimes creep in.

He still winces when he recalls the morning he stopped dead at a full-page Regal Shoe ad announcing a new store opening. Proofs had looked fine the day before, and Regal had happily O.K.'d them. The ad looked fine in the paper, too, except for one thing: In a field of what was supposed to be white space stood a can of London Street Tobacco.

The explanation was simple. A composing-room printer, assembling the tobacco ad, dropped the gum-backed tobacco tin engraving on the white area in the finished Regal plate— temporarily, he thought. When the Regal plate was wheeled away to be fitted into the page form, a second printer figured the tobacco tin engraving had purposely been gummed to the Regal ad for cutting in. He acted on that thought—and Regal turned up with tobacco in its shoes. Ragona apologized to

both advertisers. They had not suffered from the error; if anything, it attracted extra attention to their ads. Sometimes,
though, a simple apology won't do. A serious error—such as
a wrong price—can mean a rebate, or even a free rerun, for
the advertiser.

This morning there are no such glaring goofs, though by
the time he has flipped through the paper Ragona pretty well
knows what calls will be waiting for him when he reaches the
office. His trained eye spots reproduction errors—dirty or
muddy printing, for example, of an article for sale—and he
can pinpoint the irate advertisers who will be scorching his
line. His phones are never silent. He takes not only the sizzlers
but several hundred others each day from advertisers and
agencies. Some want reports on ad progress; others want advice on how to prepare their material for best possible display
in The Times. And there are always a number of advertisers
who—no matter how perfect the reproduction—had expected
or fondly dreamed they might get something better. Ragona, a
patient man, has all the answers.

                                                    • • •

Five thousand miles away in Moscow, Henry Kamm, to his
surprise and pleasure, is getting the answers to his questions
from the House of Culture lady in the Ukraine. His interpreter, Boris, has gotten through to her on the telephone and
is asking the questions Kamm had framed in what he considered the unlikely event the call would be completed. The lady
denies the charges leveled against her by *Pravda* and, through
Boris, extends an invitation to Kamm to visit the Ukrainian
town and see for himself how culture is flourishing there.
Kamm makes a note to ask the Foreign Ministry for permission to make the trip. It would be a nice little story. Then he
bundles himself against the biting cold and walks briskly out
of the building. He is saluted by the ever-present policeman
who guards the entrance and records all goings and comings.
He heads for the American Embassy for the weekly 4 P.M.

briefing by the chargé d'affaires. The briefing doesn't yield much hard news, but Kamm is interested to note that the chargé is much less confident than he had been that there will be no Communist-sparked crisis over the West German elections coming up in West Berlin.

• • •

As the clocks in the empty newsroom in New York read 7:15 A.M., the Nixon press plane taxis to a stop at Orly Airport in Paris. It's 1:15 in the afternoon, and the President's plane, Air Force One, is not scheduled to touch down for forty-five minutes. Nothing for Frankel, Semple and the rest of the press corps to do but stomp around and try to keep warm. De Gaulle arrives in a small Citroen. "This fellow's carrying austerity too far," Semple whispers to Frankel, and they wonder how the General's long legs fit into the thing. Air Force One arrives. Nixon looks out the window, sees de Gaulle without a coat and sheds his own. The President also notices that de Gaulle has no text, and stuffs his into his pocket. A good thing, too, Frankel and Semple agree. His prepared remarks were embarrassingly flattering to the General. The press had read them when they were handed out on the plane. "It's fine to be nice to the General," Semple commented, "but not obsequious." But Nixon does not read the text. He speaks extemporaneously, and the effusive phrases of the original are missing. We're robbed of a story, Semple thinks, but our pride is restored. De Gaulle's little speech is gracious and warm.

Nixon and de Gaulle, followed by the press buses, leave Orly and drive into Paris. At the Quai d'Orsay, de Gaulle says farewell and Nixon retires to his apartment for half an hour. The press buses go on to the Arc de Triomphe to await Nixon's arrival for the traditional wreath-laying ceremony on the Tomb of the Unknown Soldier. Semple and Frankel hop out and walk to the nearby Hotel Georges Cinq, press headquarters for the tour, to park their luggage and freshen up.

Paris bureau members have watched the arrival and motorcade on the office TV. Henry Tanner decided that since Frankel and Semple were with the Nixon party, there was no reason to send any of his men into the massive traffic jams that piled up at the airport and along the route because of the unusually heavy security measures. Tanner knew that if anything unforeseen occurred during the drive into town, The Times was well covered. When Nixon retired into the Quai d'Orsay, Tanner decided it was time for a break and ordered coffee for all hands from the café downstairs.

• • •

In Israel, Robert Finch, Nixon's Secretary of Health, Education and Welfare, and the American delegation he has led to the Eshkol funeral wait to be received by Acting Premier Yigal Allon. Jim Feron is waiting, too. The foyer of Allon's office is full of big men—bigger than Feron, who is of medium height—and it occurs to him that he keeps forgetting how short Israelis are until a batch of Americans show up. He is introduced to Joseph Cisco, the American Undersecretary of State for Middle East Affairs. This is the man he'd like to talk to, but at that moment a secretary ushers the delegation into Allon's office. Feron unobtrusively melts into the group and starts toward the office, but a hand on his shoulder stops him. It's the director of Jerusalem's Public Information Office. "You can't go in, Jim. It's off the record." No amount of fast-talking can get him through the door. He climbs into his car and drives home. It was a nice try.

• • •

In Kenya, Larry Fellows is still waiting in his car at the bank of the Athi River, hoping for a vehicle of some kind to come from the opposite direction to show that the road beyond the river has not been washed out by the rain. He's somewhat startled to see a Masai warrior emerge from the bush, his body painted with red ocher and dung, his hair plaited into a fanciful peruke with dozens of strings hanging from it like candlewicks. His only clothing is a piece of stained calico draped over his shoulders. Among other things he doesn't wear are trousers.

Fellows greets the warrior casually with the Masai greeting, "Sopa," the only word he knows of the language. The warrior stops, leans his elbows on the hood of the car and starts talking; but Fellows can't follow him, though it's obvious the man recognizes him. Suddenly it comes clear—they had once Indian wrestled and Fellows had won; the Masai wants a return engagement. Fellows gets slowly out of the car, recalling the advice he had received before their first encounter: Most Masai have underdeveloped forearms and so are pushovers in an Indian wrestle. They lock fingers. Fellows, a strong, wiry young man, quickly bends back the warrior's wrist, and the victory is his. The Masai dives back into the bush.

Before Fellows can get back into his car, it is pouring rain. The little Athi River begins to swell and rush with muddy water. Fellows gives up the idea of going to Kajiado to interview the Indian trader. He turns his car around and starts back to Nairobi.

As he dashes through the rain to his office in the *East African Standard* building, he collides with Kamau, his messenger. Kamau, who belongs to a Bantu-speaking agricultural tribe, is beaming. Fellows, shaking himself off, asks what's so wonderful about getting soaked. "Lain, Lain," Kamau says, pronouncing r's like l's. "Mingi mzuri," he adds in crude Swahili, which Fellows, whose Swahili is also crude, understands to mean "Very good."

Fellows decides to write a story about the rain; but before he can start to write, he has to get a lot more information than he now has. He girds himself for the battle with the telephone. He finally gets through to the Meteorological Department and learns that it is raining all over East Africa. The department spokesman tells him that though most of the advance signs were missing, these are definitely the Long

Rains. He calls an English farmer he knows in Kiambu to ask how the rains are affecting his crops. The farmer reports he is sitting pretty because he has sprayed all his coffee trees. Coffee? This is a wrinkle that had not occurred to Fellows. The farmer explains that to beat coffee berry disease, which hit Kenya hard two years earlier, the coffee crop must be sprayed with fungicide in dry weather, before the rains start. This year three-quarters of the coffee crop is being produced by Africans, and a setback for them could be a disaster for the country. Fellows must find out if the Africans had the foresight to protect their crops.

He calls a friend on the Coffee Marketing Board, who expresses grave concern. The feeling at the board is that practically no coffee growers had sprayed their trees because the rains had not been expected for another month. A call to the Coffee Research Station at Ruiru reveals the fear that the spread of coffee berry disease will get out of control. Fellows's story is building with every call.

• • •

Across the African continent, R. W. (Johnny) Apple, Jr., and his wife have just reached Lagos, Nigeria, which is to be his operational base for the next few months. The Apples had flown the West African milk run from Dakar (Senegal) to Roberts Field (Liberia) to Accra (Ghana) and thence to Lagos, a five-and-half-hour flight on which they had inklings of what life in Africa was going to be like. At the Accra airport they had gotten off the plane marveling at the shiny new terminal building, and were directed to a tiny, sweltering shack alongside. They were informed that the new terminal had been opened to celebrate the anniversary of the overthrow of the dictatorial Kwame Nkrumah, then hastily closed. Why, the Apples wondered? But they got no answer. They bought a magazine from a small, barefooted vendor about eight years old, and asked for change in something more convertible than Ghanaian money. The wise moppet offered the suggestion that the Apples could drink up the change at the bar before their flight left. They did.

Finally, Lagos. They got through customs with no problems only to have their taxi halted outside the airport by a fierce-looking soldier. Kneeling on the broiling asphalt pavement, Apple opened their luggage and patiently explained why they had so many books, when and where they bought their small radio, until the soldier became bored and let them pass. Apple discovered later that what the soldier wanted was "dash"—the West African term for a bribe—but he hadn't learned that yet. At about 2:30 P.M. they wheezed into town in their ancient taxi, checked into the Hilton Federal Palace Hotel and ordered dessicated chicken sandwiches from room service. The waiting mail revealed that the office car had only three usable tires and its insurance had lapsed, and that the cook had decamped with the key to the front door of The Times's house. All this will wait, Apple figures. He sends off a cable to Topping: ARRIVED LAGOS HOPE START FILING MONDAY ALL WELL REGARDS—and throws himself on the bed for a nap.

· · ·

But there was no napping 275 miles to the east, in Umuahia, capital of the breakaway Nigerian province of Biafra, now in the twentieth month of a miserable, devastating civil war. Lloyd Garrison, tall, handsome, intrepid, had been stationed in Nigeria before and during the early days of secession. He had been expelled in 1967 by the central government, which looked upon his reporting from Biafra as "an unfriendly act." Now he has come back—from Paris—to write some articles about the cruel reality of life in Biafra today. Logically, he knows the Nigerian civil war should not involve a reporter's emotions—but involve him it does, if only out of the horror of civilian suffering, especially the suffering of the children who die by the hundreds every day.

Garrison had arisen at 7 o'clock in one of the bungalows of the Progress Hotel, the town's tin-roofed, ramshackle inn. No running water this morning; therefore, no bath or shave. He heated some coffee in the kerosene stove, drank a can of V-8 juice, then set out to take pictures for a "Talk of Umuahia" piece he was working on, the profile-of-a-city-type story that The Times frequently carries. He focused on the outdoor market and on the main street; and as he pointed his camera at a Biafran policewoman directing traffic, he got a toothy smile in return. He liked that picture and hoped it would be selected by the picture desk in New York to illustrate the story. (He was pleased to learn later that it was.)

He stops by the Overseas Press Center to send a cable to the foreign desk in New York informing them that the film will be carried out of the country tonight by a *Time* magazine reporter and can be picked up in a day or two at *Time*'s office in New York.

There is a loud bang, something like a backfire, and everyone in the Center dives for cover under the concrete stairwell. There is no warning system in Biafra. No sirens announce a Nigerian air raid; the first hint that a raid is in progress comes from the boom of Biafran guns that ring the hills around Umuahia.

But this time nothing happens. It probably *was* a backfire, Garrison decides, or perhaps a door slamming in the wind. He knows that if the Egyptian-piloted jets from Nigeria have failed to show up by noon, the knot of fear that everyone in Umuahia wakes up with begins to wear off. They almost always bomb before lunch.

So he emerges from under the stairwell and walks to the World Council of Churches' headquarters, dodging the bunkers and slit shelter trenches that pit the town. At 1 P.M., feeling that perhaps at least for today the danger is passed, he is nursing an ice-cold glass of filtered water as he interviews WCC representatives. At 1:05 there is no mistaking the boom of

Biafran guns. Garrison and the men he is talking with dash out the door and scramble into a bunker. They look up to see a MIG bomber coming in low, guns chattering. It seems to Garrison that it is strafing the Progress Hotel, which not only houses journalists but is the well-marked headquarters of the Red Cross. Two bombs fall; both explode in the bush about half a mile from the bunker.

And then, seconds later, it is over. The men drag themselves from the bunker, dust themselves off and go back inside the building. Garrison's legs are shaking; he's glad he's wearing fatigues instead of short pants. Everybody laughs and drinks ice water and makes small talk to cover up.

Later in the afternoon, Garrison learns that the strafing was one hundred yards up the hill "just behind Jaggi's place." Harry Jaggi is the Swiss head of the International Red Cross.

• • •

Managing Editor Clifton Daniel had felt grippy and feverish when he turned in last night after reading the first edition of The Times, which had been dropped off at his Park Avenue apartment about 10:30. First editions, hot off the press, are delivered each night to the homes of a dozen or so top editors. It gives them a head start on their reading. It also gives them a chance to call the night editors to suggest changes for editions still to be printed.

As Lloyd Garrison crouches in the Biafran bunker, Daniel's alarm goes off. It's 7:45. Sleep has not dissipated the grippy feeling. He'll have to stay home today; his secretary will call him if anything urgent that requires an immediate decision comes up. Daniel is primarily an administrator. He copes with the personnel problems affecting the 900 men and women in the news department. He goes through stacks of reader mail, pruning it for ideas and for any pattern of criticism that might run through it. Each day he sees a procession of visitors, many of them applicants for jobs, many of them outsiders seeking favors from The Times or registering disagreements with it.

Today, though, he is feeling miserable.

• • •

In Paris Paul Hofmann is feeling miserable, too. He is in the French capital on temporary duty, on loan from the local news staff in New York to cover the Vietnam peace talks. This is a full-time assignment right now, and the Paris bureau would find itself short-staffed if one of its reporters were to cover the talks to the exclusion of everything else. The sessions themselves are not so time-consuming. It's the digging for what goes on behind the scenes, the news that is not included in the official handouts, that keeps Hofmann hopping. A Viennese, a linguist, urbane and cosmopolitan, he can match diplomats at their own game.

At 2 o'clock this afternoon he is walking along the Boulevard Haussmann on his way to the dentist for the extraction of an impacted wisdom tooth. He had plotted the date carefully. Friday is an anticlimactic day on his beat because the weekly plenary sessions are held on Thursday. Furthermore, President Nixon, at this moment arriving in Paris, is not due to be briefed on the Vietnam talks until Sunday. So today shapes up as the ideal day for the long-deferred extraction.

To get into the right stoical spirit and, at the same time, cultivate his sources, Hofmann had met for lunch with three Vietnam neutralists, neutral in that they support neither Hanoi and the Vietcong nor the Saigon regime. The talk turned naturally to the progress of the peace talks. Hofmann learned from his companions that members of the North Vietnamese negotiating team had been observed calling repeatedly at the Soviet Embassy during the week. This tip added to a growing volume of circumstantial evidence that Soviet diplomacy was again involved in the talks, as it had been at previous stages of the negotiations. He'd do some checking.

First, though, the extraction. But the dentist's equipment breaks down just as he starts his grisly work. Reprieved, Hofmann hustles to the bureau on rue Caumartin to pursue the Soviet Embassy tip with telephone calls across Paris to diplomats of various nations.

Out of his calls comes another tip. More calls, more checking, finally, confirmation: Nixon will meet with Vice President Nguyen Cao Ky of South Vietnam during his stay in Paris.

He has a good story for tomorrow's paper.

𝕾 𝖆.𝖒.

The Times's plant on 43d Street begins to stir.

In the subbasement pressroom clean-up crews sweep tons of paper from the concrete floor and wipe away the ink, oil, paper dust—leftovers from last night's press run. Maintenance crews weave in and out among the great machines, tuning up the intricate mechanisms to make sure everything is mechanically perfect for tonight's run. A breakdown in the pressroom can cause nervous breakdowns throughout the plant, for the combined daily toil of 6,000 Times men and women is void and without form until it leaps at dizzying speed from the presses.

In the wire room on the third floor, adjacent to the newsroom, clerks strip overnight copy and messages from the teleprinter machines, run them off on duplicators and drop them through a chute to the "slot" boys, who sort them and distribute them to the news desk that will handle them. There are six major news desks—foreign, national, metropolitan, sports, financial-business and culture—and each desk handles the news its name implies.

The vast newsroom sprawls over 1⅓ acres. It is filled with hundreds of gray, metal-topped desks, arranged in a phalanx that impresses visitors—who seem to expect something like the set from *The Front Page*—as being more like an insurance office than a newsroom. Its walls are freshly painted. Its low, well-lit ceiling is supported by brightly colored pillars.

The managing editor's office and the desks of the major editors—the associate managing editor, three assistant managing editors and the news editors—line the south wall. A few feet to the north are desk clusters occupied by the foreign, national and metropolitan editors and their assistants and nearby are their horseshoe-shaped copydesks. Beyond, the 300-odd reporters' desks stretch north, row upon row, to the far reaches of the room. The subsidiary departments—sports, financial-business news and culture—are self-contained units set off by partitions.

The floor is almost deserted at 8 A.M. The senior man on duty is John Dugan, the picture assignment editor. He flips through early agency copy to make sure nothing has come up during the night that requires picture coverage. Events scheduled in advance had been assigned as "overnights"; the photographers had been instructed last evening to report directly to the scene of the event.

                                                        • • •

Dugan's seniority holds only until 8:15 when James (Scotty) Reston shows up. Scotty (the name traces to his Scottish birthplace) has never acquired morning newspaper habits, at least as far as office hours are concerned. He finds the early morning a good time to read through papers other than The Times —this morning, for example, he gets through *The Washington Post,* the *Los Angeles Times, The Wall Street Journal* and *Women's Wear.* He goes through his mail and the memos that have piled up, and makes and takes telephone calls in his three-room office suite on the newsroom floor.

This morning he taps out messages on his electric typewriter to Max Frankel and Anthony Lewis, complimenting them on their stories about the Nixon tour. FRANKEL REPORT EXCELLENT ALL WEEK STOP PLEASE PAY MY RESPECTS ALL CONCERNED. This message greets Frankel in the Paris bureau when he reaches there from Rome. To

Lewis, Reston cables: GRAND JOB ON NIXON ALL AROUND. Lewis finds the message on his desk when he returns from lunch at London's famous Garrick Club.

· · ·

Six floors above the newsroom, Jean Hewitt, The Times's home economist, is cooking up a sweet-smelling storm in the ninth-floor test kitchen, where all recipes are prepared and tasted before they are served to readers of the women's page. Mrs. Hewitt, with her shoulder-length brown hair and chic designer suit, protected by a large apron, looks like a fashion model. But the aromas emanating from the kitchen prove that she is also a cook. The kitchen occupies more space than most home kitchens—it was designed with extremely wide floor space to allow for photographers to set up lights and cameras —but in every other respect it is a home-type kitchen rather than the restaurant or hotel sort, and all the cooking and baking done in it are measured in home quantities.

This morning Mrs. Hewitt is melting chocolate and heating cream, the basic ingredients of a frosting for a Sacher Torte and a Poppy Seed Torte she baked yesterday. She is testing the recipes in a new Viennese cookbook before she presents them to readers. At the same time her oven is aglow with a filet of beef. Later in the morning the filet, garnished with artichoke bottoms and green peas—light-colored vegetables to provide snap and contrast—will sit for its portrait. The meat platter will appear as a "New York Times Magazine" food-page feature on Sunday. Once they have been photographed, the dishes will end up as unannounced bonuses in The Times's cafeteria for employes.

· · ·

Though it will be hours before the newsroom reaches peak activity, the pursuit of news in New York City and throughout the country is under way. Vartanig Vartan, the slight, bald financial writer, is finishing The Times and *The Wall Street Journal,* part of his background reading for the daily stock-market lead he puts together each night. An item in the *Journal* stops him: the suggestion by the president of the New York Stock Exchange that the Big Board is considering delisting the shares of two conglomerate companies. Vartan knows this could mean trouble on the Exchange. The market has been falling sharply for two weeks, and Wall Street is sensitive to any piece of adverse news. Furthermore, conglomerate stocks were weak yesterday. He'll keep an eye on how they react today.

• • •

Art Critic John Canaday, after a sleepless night, is approaching Kennedy Airport to catch an 8:50 A.M. plane for Dayton, Ohio, to gather material for an article for Sunday's "Arts and Leisure" section on the Dayton Art Institute's fiftieth anniversary celebration. The art critic's job is a roving one—he must keep up on trends, developments and innovations wherever they may be exhibited. As his taxi passes what is left of the New York World's Fair grounds, Canaday thinks about the stories he wrote on the Fair five years ago. He reflects upon the fact that he had called the unisphere a "permanent disfigurement," and that it is still there disfiguring like crazy.

• • •

In New Orleans, where it is one hour earlier than New York, Martin Waldron—a paunchy, rumpled bear of a man—awakens at 7, yawning and regretting that he ate too much chili the evening before. He prepares to cover the trial of Clay L. Shaw, the man accused by New Orleans District Attorney Jim Garrison of plotting the murder of President Kennedy. The trial, now in its sixth week, is rapidly drawing to a close. Today, as a matter of fact, may close it out. Waldron, who normally works out of Houston, has rented an apartment in the city's French Quarter for the trial's duration. This morning he makes himself a breakfast of scrambled eggs, sirloin steak, Parker House rolls, coffee and orange juice. He wants to fortify himself against the possibility that he may have to pass up lunch, even dinner, should the trial reach a climax close to an edition deadline.

· 9 a.m.

All foreign correspondents have the problem of living in two worlds of time—the foreign desk's in New York, and their own. This is particularly tough in Vietnam, where it is thirteen hours later than New York. If they're lucky and it has been a quiet day, they will get their copy to the telegraph office by 11 P.M. This gives them an hour for a bite to eat or a nightcap before the midnight curfew. More often, though, they're at their typewriters well past midnight and have to summon a military jeep to escort them to the telegraph office six blocks away.

So now, at 10 P.M.—as their colleagues in New York start the day—the staff in Saigon is pounding out copy for the first edition of tomorrow's paper. There will still be time tomorrow morning to freshen up, for late editions, what they write tonight. Terry Smith is well into his summary of the day's military action: "Enemy gunners shelled about 30 military and civilian targets around South Vietnam today while five companies of American infantrymen fought a day-long battle six miles from the center of Saigon." Then he wraps in the details of the suburban fighting that Treaster has supplied.

Charlie Mohr, refreshed by a bath and a good meal, is writing about his experiences last night at the fire-support base forty miles northwest of Saigon. He decides to build his story

around some of the relatively new firepower developments—
among them something called Killer Junior—that help keep
Americans alive when the Vietcong attack. He slugs the story
"Junior," the word that will identify it as it moves across the
world by radio and cable—first to Hong Kong, from there to
London and thence across the Atlantic to Times Square. He
bats out 800 words explaining that Killer Junior is a variety
of 105 millimeter shell with a time fuse that gives an airburst
at predetermined distances, throwing shrapnel in lethal patterns on the ground below.

Tonight their stories are at the telegraph office well before
curfew. Mohr has a nightcap and turns in. Smith has dinner
and returns to the office to write a weekender for Sunday's
"Week in Review" section. At 1:30 in the morning he calls for
a military escort for the spooky drive through the deserted
streets. Then it's lights out for him, too.

. . .

In Nairobi, Larry Fellows is also at the typewriter. He has
worked the telephone to round up the effects of the early rains
on Kenya's economically vital coffee crop. Now he's ready to
put his findings on paper. There is still a chance that the rains
will falter and set in again when they are due, a month later,
but the chance is slim. He decides to lead his story with at
least a hint of the disaster the coffee growers fear. He writes:

"From the edge of the northern desert to the slopes and
ridges before Lake Tanganyika comma the long rains have arrived in East Africa comma bearing the faint smell of agricultural disaster."

Before the sun sets over East Africa, his copy has started
toward New York by telex, the normal filing method for correspondents in Africa and most of Europe. It is also the cheap-
est; it is charged by the minute, whereas telegraph copy is
charged by the word. There is a telex machine in the *East African Standard,* where Fellows has his office. He hands his
story to the operator, who dials the London bureau's telex

number on a telephonelike dial attached to the machine, then punches the copy on the machine's keyboard. It goes to London over regular telegraph lines, materializing in the form of punched tape, and from London to New York by cable. Fellows, meanwhile, can check the print-out at the sending end for accuracy.

Fellows is lucky. Many correspondents outside the sophisticated world capitals do not have access to telex machines and must carry their copy to local telegraph offices. Though communications are generally better than they used to be, they are still spotty and, in some places, primitive. This creates a terrible problem for reporters, who know that the best story in the world is no good until it reaches the editor's desk. Telegraph offices in Africa lean toward chaos. The single overworked operator is frequently too tired or too busy to send the copy even if one of the limited lines outside the country is available. Paul Hofmann, who did a tour of duty in East Africa a few years ago, described the occupational disease of correspondents as "tropical telex neurosis." Its symptoms, he said, were "severe anxiety after, say, a four-hour wait for the line, and a tendency to jockey and bribe for priority."

• • •

Max Frankel and Bob Semple are freshening up in their luxurious suite in the elegant Hotel Georges Cinq in Paris. Champagne on ice has greeted their arrival. There had been nothing like this earlier in the trip; it had been too fast and hectic for any such amenities. But with a whole week end in Paris, maybe the pace will let up a bit. Semple hopes so. It's his first trip abroad since he went as a student fifteen years ago, and so far he can't say he's seen anything except airports, ceremonies, press rooms. "Paris," he thinks to himself as he showers. "The Georges Cinq! Hemingway used to drink here." Perhaps he'll even get some time off, if Tanner does the story tonight.

The question of who would write today's story had arisen on the plane from Rome. Frankel, as traveling bureau chief and maitre d' of the tour, has sought throughout the trip to balance his own desire to write, Semple's desire to write, and the desires of the various foreign bureau members to participate in the story. Things have evened up fairly well. In London, which was typical, Semple did the story one day, Anthony Lewis the next, and Frankel supplied Q-heads, the house term for "think," or news analysis, pieces. Frankel's idea for today is that Tanner write the story of Nixon's arrival, incorporating the French point of view toward the upcoming talks. But he won't decide definitely until he has talked it over with Tanner. The car and chauffeur that have been hired to tote him and Semple around Paris is on its way to the hotel to pick them up and take them to the bureau. It's a little after 3 P.M., but it's just past 9 A.M. in New York—plenty of time to work out today's schedule.

. . .

The early starters have begun to trickle into the 43d Street newsroom, carrying, almost without exception, the inevitable paper coffee container. On the foreign desk, David Andelman, the news clerk, is summarizing for Seymour Topping's attention the foreign news that has occurred since the paper closed at 3 A.M.

"In the news this morning," he writes, "Nixon leaves Rome and arrives in Paris. . . . Premier Levi Eshkol is buried on Mt. Herzl. . . . In Viet, 30 towns and bases shelled overnight. . . . Strong earthquake hits Portugal and Morocco."

The foreign desk phone jangles. Pan American's press relations department is on the line. Pan Am has heard the radio report of the earthquake and is worried about its passengers in the area. What does The Times have on it? Another call: A mother whose daughter is in Morocco asks nervously how serious the earthquake is. Andelman gives them what little information he has picked up from the wire-service copy.

Armida Gaeta, the assistant to the foreign news editor, who doubles as mother-in-residence to all foreign correspondents,

checks the messages that have arrived overnight from correspondents all over the world. Those that require Topping's attention she piles neatly on his desk to await his arrival. Many
of them are for her: messages to be delivered to relatives in
New York; snafus to be untangled in the accounting department; requests for vitamin tablets, curtain material or whatever else is not at the correspondent's hand. All their personal
problems are Miss Gaeta's, and she never lets them down.

By 9:30 she has assembled all the data relating to correspondents who are away from their home bases and has turned
it over to a desk clerk who will type the Daily Listing of Foreign Correspondents' Movements, for distribution to all the
newsroom editors. The national and metropolitan desks com-
pile similar lists of their staff's movements so that all editors
know precisely where everybody is on a given day. The foreign desk list this morning notes that Frankel and Semple can
be reached at the Paris bureau, which will come as a surprise
to no one, and also includes the not so generally known fact
that Malcolm W. Browne, correspondent in Buenos Aires, is
at the Hotel Crillon in Santiago, Chile, where he has gone to
cover the congressional elections; and that Tad Szulc, who is
based in Vienna, is at the Athenée Palace Hotel in Bucharest
to cover the upcoming Rumanian elections.

• • •

Szulc had reached Bucharest seven hours earlier after an overnight train trip from Vienna. He had planned to fly, but
planes had been grounded for two days in Eastern Europe by
blustery weather. Train travel across the Balkans, he found,
was an education on how each Socialist country worries about
smuggling from another Socialist country. Yugoslavia, he discovered, had beautiful, well-coiffed blondes in uniform as customs inspectors. Rumania did not.

Polish-born Szulc is on his first visit to Rumania and does
not speak the language. His first act, upon reaching his hotel,
is to hire an interpreter to help him through the newspapers

and other documents that he needs for background on the election. Then he calls on the Foreign Office press division, which arranges for him to attend the final pre-election speech by President Nicholae Ceausescu later in the day.

As the Listing of Foreign Correspondents' Movements is distributed to the various news desks in New York, Szulc arrives at the Great Hall of the National Palace to hear Ceausescu. The Rumanians, eager for international coverage, put him in a loge with other foreign newsmen and give him a headset for simultaneous interpretation into four languages. He'll be comfortable, at least, while the 102-minute speech drones on.

. . .

On the national desk, a few feet from the foreign desk, Irvin Horowitz, an assistant editor, is the early man. He finds less of an overnight pileup than the foreign desk because national bureaus, unlike overseas bureaus, operate either in the same time zone as New York's or an earlier one.

He sends a memo to the accounting department authorizing payment to three stringers—part-time correspondents who are paid by the number of words they write—for pieces they filed yesterday.

"Pl. credit Julie Kennedy, U. of Wisconsin, with $30 for a report on a rampage at the University.

"Pls. credit Jack Bass with $25 for a report on a legislative call for a program to deal with hunger in South Carolina.

"Pls. credit Win Rockwell, Dartmouth College, with $10 for a report on a new dean."

. . .

At the metropolitan desk, adjacent to the national desk, Gil Haggerty, a news assistant, goes through the wire copy that has piled up since 3 A.M. and marks it for the "beat" man who will handle it.

Most of the activity in the newsroom at 9 A.M. takes place around the mail boxes, where the mail clerk, assisted by four copyboys, is sorting the morning mail, stuffing it into slots marked with the names of each editor, reporter and copy-reader. Haggerty's pile of wire copy goes into the slots of the men for whom it is designated.

· · ·

Philip H. Dougherty, who writes the daily advertising column for the business pages, is riding the jam-packed subway from his home in Forest Hills, Queens, toward Madison Avenue, the heart of the world's advertising community. The ad crowd starts cracking early; so, perforce, does Dougherty.

The first stop of his day is 666 Fifth Avenue, where he has a 9:30 appointment with Arthur E. Duram, president of Fuller & Smith & Ross, the advertising agency that helped put President Nixon in the White House. Dougherty arrives at 9:15 to find Duram waiting. But before talk there is coffee. There is always coffee. It helps the juices flow. Dougherty has two cups.

He is working ahead, as he must, to turn out six columns a week. It will be seven days before he uses Duram. He puts his questions, scribbles down the answers—some biographical stuff, a bit of history of the agency, what it was like to handle a Presidential candidate, how the future looks. Later in the morning, Bart Silverman, a Times photographer, will stop by to catch Duram on film, but Dougherty will be gone by then. He has two other agency men to see before an early lunch with a third.

· · ·

In Washington, the day begins earlier for bureau members than it does for most of the New York staff. The departments of Government, a major element in the Washington news report, are early starters and so, therefore, are the men who cover them. This morning, Benjamin Welles, whose beat includes the State Department and the Embassy run, is off to a miserable beginning. The tall, distinguished-looking son of former Under Secretary of State Sumner Welles has awakened red-eyed and bilious, wracked by the Washington flu. But he faces a busy morning, and he cannot yield to his misery. Last night Harold Gal, an assistant news editor in the bureau, had proposed that Welles prepare a "Man in the News" profile on John Freeman, due to arrive in Washington the next Monday as British Ambassador. These profiles of people in the news are a daily Times feature. Sometimes the subject emerges out of a spot-news story and the sketch must be put together hard on deadline, mainly from clippings in the newspaper's morgue. Frequently, though, as in the case of Freeman, a "Man in the News" can be forecast, thus giving the reporter more time to assemble material that provides an indication of character and personality rather than straight biography.

Welles has a 9:30 appointment at the British Embassy to get background material on Freeman. He purposely made it early so he could get to the office to finish up a "Week in Review" piece on Latin America that should have been in New York last night. His first Embassy contact has little to offer; he had served under Freeman for only two weeks years ago. His next contact is more fruitful, and Welles hastily scribbles pages of notes. Then he grabs his hat and coat from an Embassy attendant and tries, in vain, to whistle down a cab. By the time he reaches The Times's bureau, his misery is compounded by rage. He had waited eighteen minutes for a bus.

Warming Up

· · · · 10 a.m.

The Times's Washington bureau—an elegant, carpeted, floor-through suite of offices on the eighth floor of a new building in the northwest section of the capital—is the newspaper's largest outpost. Its sixty men and women include twenty-seven reporters and editors, one editorial writer and two editorial page columnists, two Sunday department representatives, two photographers, two librarians, secretaries, wire-room operators, clerks and copyboys.

Max Frankel, the bureau chief, has organized his reporters in clusters, a slight variation of the old-fashioned beat where each man covered a building (the White House, the Pentagon, the State Department) or a specific field (economics, civil rights, foreign affairs). Under the cluster system, specialists in related fields—civil rights, housing and the Department of Health, Education and Welfare, for example—meet with Frankel a couple of times a week to exchange information and ideas. Each man in a cluster is competent to backstop and fill in for the others, no matter from what Government building or department the news emanates. Frankel believes that the cluster system, by merging fields of interest, makes for more meaningful and less isolated coverage and, just as important, adds to each reporter's understanding of his area of the news. Although the trend in all newspaper reporting is toward specialization, nowhere has it become so finely honed as in Washington, where almost every reporter is a specialist.

In immediate charge of assigning reporters and editing what they turn in is Robert H. Phelps, the bureau news editor, and his assistants. They make sure each day that a man is at the spot where significant news is breaking, or may break. In consultation with the man on the beat, they decide which events merit special attention and which are routine and can be handled by the wire services.

Now, at 10 A.M., Phelps and David Jones, his first assistant, are at the news desk reading the messages that have passed between 43d Street and the bureau since they went home last night at 7:30. Jones looks through the summary of stories from *The Washington Post,* which a clerk has prepared for his attention. No need, he's relieved to learn, to try to recoup on anything there. The phone jangles; reporters are checking in from Government bureaus all over the city. William Beecher, who covers military affairs, calls from the Pentagon. He tells Phelps that he is about ready to write a major story predicting what course the Defense Department will take on the controversial antiballistic missile issue. He outlines the story over the phone. Since this comes under planned news as opposed to spot news—the report of day-to-day events—Phelps suggests that Beecher write it for Sunday's paper rather than Saturday's, because of the larger Sunday audience.

Marjorie Hunter, a Capitol Hill reporter, calls from the Senate press gallery to propose that she spend the day in the office of Senator Ernest F. Hollings of South Carolina going through mail he has received from his constituents following a speech he made on hunger in South Carolina. Phelps gives her the go-ahead; he has nothing for her on the schedule, and he knows where he can reach her should a spot story develop on the Hill.

Nona Brown, the Sunday department's Washington representative, has arrived in the bureau, fingers crossed as usual on

Friday morning, hoping that not everybody has waited until today to file pieces ordered from New York by Robert Clurman, "The Week in Review" editor, for Sunday's section. These pieces, which summarize, analyze and provide the background of the major events of the week, are due in New York on Thursday night, unless they deal with a breaking story, in which case copy can be accepted right up to the Saturday afternoon deadline. Each week Clurman fondly hopes that he will get early copy so that he can begin to lay out his section on Friday. Mrs. Brown discovers that today there are only two delinquents: Eileen Shanahan, one of the bureau's two economics experts, and Ben Welles.

Shanahan, it turns out, had arisen at 6:30 to write her piece on taxes in the basement workroom of her home. She pants into the office, thrusts her copy into Mrs. Brown's hands and pants out to catch a cab for Capitol Hill to attend a Ways and Means Committee hearing on tax reform. Welles, Mrs. Brown notes as she glances around the newsroom, is hammering away at his piece on Latin America. Inwardly he's seething, the result of an exchange with David Jones, who casually greeted him as he rushed in a few minutes ago from the British Embassy with: "Ben, forget about the Freeman profile. We just got a message from the London bureau that they're doing it."

Correspondents in Washington, as in all Government capitals, maintain close contact with the important officials who are their major news sources. Some mingle socially with Government bigwigs, and occasionally a good story develops over lunch or after-dinner coffee. A few days ago John W. Finney, a foreign-affairs specialist, had picked up a tip over lunch about an attractive offer of political patronage that President Nixon had made to Hubert Humphrey, his Democratic adversary in the recent election, if only Humphrey would become Ambassador to the United Nations. Finney tracked down the story and is now at his typewriter, writing it for Sunday's paper. This will put him in the clear to spend the afternoon at the State Department ferreting out the Russian position in the communications satellite negotiations now under way. He'll write that story this evening for tomorrow's paper.

Phelps and Jones retire into Phelps's office to confer on stories that will probably be written during the coming week. They are not talking about spot news, or running stories, but about takeouts—comprehensive stories bringing up to date or explaining a given subject—which require extended treatment. The editors in New York must know in advance what takeouts are in the works so they can figure on them in allotting space. This morning Phelps sends a list of twenty such futures now in preparation. The list includes:

Census (Nan Robertson)—A look at the plans for the 1970 census: what questions will be asked, how they were arrived at, and the current status of the invasion of privacy fight over the census.

Pentagon (Neil Sheehan)—A situation story on plans by the Pentagon to get out of the social programs that [Sec. of Defense Clark] Clifford began.

Hollings (Marjorie Hunter)—Sen. Hollings and hunger: an in-depth look at the constituent reaction, surprisingly good, to the Hollings admission of hunger in South Carolina, and why he did it.

Frankel ordinarily sits in at these morning meetings with his editors. Out of their discussions emerges a consensus of how yesterday's news was handled and what should take priority in today's. The Washington bureau has its ideas on how a story should be covered and where the emphasis should be placed but its thinking must be coordinated with that of the New York editors, who may have different ideas.

• • •

But today Frankel is 3,500 miles away in Paris. As Phelps and Jones confer in Washington, Frankel and Semple leave the

Hotel Georges Cinq in the chauffeur-driven Citroen provided by Henry Tanner and drive to the Paris bureau.

It is Semple's first visit to the bureau. As he rides the antique elevator to the fifth floor of the narrow building on rue Caumartin, he is trapped between two judgments: "How romantic!" and, "What a dump!" Certainly it is centuries away from the modern luxury of the Washington bureau to which he is accustomed. There are introductions all around, then Frankel, Semple, Tanner and John Hess go into Tanner's office to talk. The Washingtonians brief the bureau men on the trip so far and are, in turn, briefed on the attitude of the French toward Nixon. Semple steals a glance out of the window at the rooftops. On his last visit fifteen years ago, he had never inspected them at such close range. He snaps back to the talk around him when Tanner's quiet voice asks: "Well, how shall we handle today's story?" Frankel suggests that Tanner do it. Tanner suggests that Frankel or Semple do it. Frankel argues that they have written about Nixon's objectives from all the other capitals on the tour, and a piece on what the host country is looking for would make a nice change of pace. Tanner agrees, but thinks it more logical for him to write the lead story tomorrow when the French angle will be more prominent. Frankel accepts the reasoning. All eyes swing to Semple. He is the choice. He will write today's lead. Hess will handle the sidebars.

Tom Wicker, who has been covering the Nixon trip for his editorial-page column, joins the group in Tanner's office. Wicker, also out of Washington, has not been plagued with daily deadlines as have the men writing the running story. He has worked at a more leisurely pace, has been received by important officials in the countries they have visited and, out of his interviews and his instincts, has written columns reflecting on the implications of the trip.

A little before 5 P.M. the conference breaks up. Frankel

and Tanner get off a cable to Topping, a rundown of how the story will be covered tonight:

WE ARE PUTTING ALL MATERIAL IN SINGLE STORY BY SEMPLE UNLESS THE UNEXPECTED DEVELOPS. IT WILL COVER NIXON'S ARRIVAL IN PARIS, APPARENT MOTIVATIONS OF TWO SIDES, COLOR AND REFERENCE TO DEMONSTRATIONS. ADDITIONALLY WE WILL HAVE SEVERAL SHORTS ON SECURITY, SCATTERED VIOLENCE AND THE QUAI D'ORSAY SCENE. WE RECOMMEND AND SHALL SEND FIVE RELATIVELY SHORT TEXTS: NIXON'S EFFUSIVE ARRIVAL STATEMENT AS DISTRIBUTED TO PRESS AND AS ACTUALLY DELIVERED, DEGAULLE'S GREETING AND, ASSUMING WE GET THEM, EXCHANGE OF DINNER TOASTS. THE REASON FOR NIXON'S CHANGE OF TONE IN ARRIVAL WILL BE COVERED IN LEAD.

• • •

By midmorning, some editors are arriving at their desks on the third floor of the 43d Street newsroom. As they hurry into the building, they are guided by the text that gleams in golden letters from a lobby wall:

> To give the news impartially,
>> Without fear or favor,
>> Regardless of any party,
>> Sect or interest involved.

Spot news is the daily newspaper's chief concern. But more and more in recent years, as the world has become increasingly complex, the editors have learned that it is not enough simply to chronicle an election in Germany, a teacher's strike in New York, a debate in Congress or a race riot in Chicago. Readers want to know more about the "whys" of a story, the underlying trends and influences that contribute to spot news.

The Times has increasingly opened its pages to hard-eyed scrutiny of the issues behind the news flash. Where once this type of interpretive piece was the sole province of Sunday's "Week in Review" section, today the takeout, the blockbuster, the Q-head are grist for the pages of the daily paper.

Seymour Topping, who assumed the foreign editor's chair after serving as correspondent in the capitals of the Far East and Russia, is the first news editor to reach his desk. The fifty-odd correspondents on his world-wide staff are already well into their day—some into the night—and he wants to check in with them, if necessary, while there is still time for them to carry out any instructions he may have. And he doesn't want his messages or overseas telephone calls to break into their night's sleep unless the matter is urgent. Topping is a vigorous, civilized man whose aggressive energies have not been reduced by his international sophistication. He is a study in undertones—steady, quietly efficient, cool, no matter how hot the news he is handling.

This morning he gets off a flurry of cables to his men all over the world, commenting on their stories in this morning's paper. Practically all foreign correspondents broke into the business on local news staffs, where every morning their stories were there, in black and white, for all the world to read. It means a great deal to reporters to know how their work is regarded by their editors, their colleagues and their friends, and one of the most difficult psychological adjustments for a foreign correspondent is the realization that he is living and working in a void, ignorant of whether his work is good, bad or inconsequential. He writes, files, and then remains curious —except for the brief fronting cable sent out from 43d Street which tells him little more than whether his story has been printed. That doesn't satisfy his ego. Was the story lacerated by the copydesk, he wonders, or was it run more or less the way he wrote it? These are the questions that plague men thousands of miles from home, and Topping, having been one of them, knows how important it is to tell them how their stories fared.

CHEERS AND SALUTATIONS ON FINE NIXON COVERAGE, he cables Robert Doty, bureau chief in Rome. Doty's story on the anti-Nixon riots in Rome ran as a front-page sidebar to the main Nixon story in this morning's paper. Tonight, he has notified the foreign desk, he will FILE WRAP-UP OF ITALIAN-AMERICAN TALKS.

To Bernard Gwertzman, newly posted in Moscow, whose first story appeared in today's paper, Topping cables: YOU OFF TO FINE START ON MOSCOW ASSIGNMENT. THAT INTERPRETIVE PIECE ON SOVIET INTEN-TIONS PUBLISHED TODAY WAS VERY USEFUL AND WELL DONE. To Joe Treaster in Vietnam: MANY THANKS FOR EXCELLENT PRIEST STORY WHICH WELL DIS-PLAYED INSIDE WITH YOUR GOOD PHOTO.

Topping makes mental notes of the foreign news prospects for today. Nixon in Paris will probably be the lead. A related story will be the crisis in Berlin over the upcoming West Ger-man elections. The third big foreign story, as he sees it in mid-morning, will be Vietnam.

• • •

What the cable is to the foreign news editor, the telephone is to Gene Roberts, the national news editor. A confident, shy but tough North Carolinian, Roberts covered the Deep South and was Saigon bureau chief before he was brought into the home office as national news editor, responsible for spot news and in-depth coverage of the cities, towns, farms and villages of America. Besides the Washington bureau, The Times maintains permanent staffs in Philadelphia, Boston, Atlanta, Houston, Chicago, Denver, Los Angeles and San Francisco. It also has on call more than 400 stringers, who send in items from their local communities from time to time. All this and the copy-desk that edits the output—some 300,000 words a day—are Gene Roberts's responsibility.

He and his assistants are on the phone most of the morning, calling and accepting calls from staff men all over the country, discussing the day's assignments. Irv Horowitz, his early man, has already talked with David Jones in the Washington bureau and gotten a tentative rundown of stories that will be filed from there. Out of these conversations the day's national news report begins to take shape. The list is mimeographed and distributed to all newsroom editors. It includes these breaking stories:

Sirhan trial—Douglas Robinson and Lacey Fosburgh—Los Angeles

Shaw trial—Martin Waldron—New Orleans

Pueblo hearing—Bernard Weinraub—Coronado, Cal.

Apollo 9—Richard Lyons, Houston; Walter Sullivan and John Wilford, Cape Kennedy

· · ·

At 10:25, a coiled wire of a man bursts into the newsroom— Arthur Gelb, the tall, Talmudic-looking metropolitan editor who peers from behind thick lenses as though always expecting something absolutely terrific to happen. He strides to his desk, where his assistants—Robert Alden, Marvin Siegel and Michael Stern—are going over the assignment schedule that Alden prepared the night before from the "future" folders, the metropolitan desk's daybooks.

Any advance information on a news event scheduled for a specific day is put into the basic future folder. This constantly expanding file bulges with items and ideas for today's attention, some of which have been stuffed into it as long ago as a year. It includes memos turned in by reporters, ideas that occurred to the metropolitan editor or his assistants, listings of today's events, and handouts.

Handouts, or publicity releases, which pile up on the metropolitan desk by the hundreds each day, must be winnowed thoroughly if the reader is not to be imposed upon. Those containing purely personal publicity are thrown out, and those announcing legitimate news events go into the basic future file. Another folder, labeled "Second Front," includes twenty or thirty ideas for feature stories in various stages of development, fodder for the split page, the first page of the second section. Another folder, identified as "Special Projects," holds story ideas that reporters have been working on over a period of time; another lists important birthdays and anniversaries of distinguished people, which provide news pegs for interviews. These folders and lists are scrutinized each day by the assignment editor, and everything that calls for immediate coverage is noted on his schedule. Then he matches up the reporters he has available with the stories that appear on the schedule.

Gelb and his assistants gaze across the sea of metal-topped reporters' desks that stretch fifty yards to the north. An office wag once gave Gelb a pair of binoculars to bring the outlying members of his staff into close range. His desk is also equipped with a loud-speaker, through which he and his aides can summon reporters from remote corners of the newsroom.

At 10:30 in the morning most of the reporters' desks are empty. District men are on the job at police headquarters in the city and suburbs. Beat men are at City Hall, the Municipal Building, the important courts and other public offices that generate local news. Reporters assigned to special fields— politics, civil rights, labor, housing, city and state finances— are ferreting out stories in their fields. General assignment reporters—men and women who cover city news that doesn't flow from regularly predictable sources—have either received their assignments the night before or have not yet reported in.

The local news staff is organized with the intention of having a reporter assigned to every point or field of activity which originates a considerable volume of news. Most of the 150 reporters on the local, or metropolitan, staff are beat men, specialists assigned to a certain government department or certain field of interest and responsible for the news generating therefrom.

The nitty-gritty of local news—disasters, riots, crimes, five-alarm fires—is called police news because the metropolitan desk usually finds out about it from the police department. The telegraph bureau at police headquarters reports hundreds of incidents every day. Most of them are trivial—"man slips and breaks leg in front of 55 East 76 St."—but to make sure that all incidents of significance are covered, reporters at police headquarters sift through the avalanche of bulletins and flash the desk immediately if a slip carries something of major importance or a clue to a possible story. Then a general assignment reporter is dispatched from the office to the scene.

General assignment reporters are the backbone of the local news staff. This mobile reserve of reporter-writers have a grasp of their craft and their city that enables them, at a moment's notice, to invade any field and turn out a competent, readable story.

Gelb had been consulted last evening as today's schedule was being made up, but this morning he sits down with his assistants to make sure everything that must be covered has been assigned and add assignments that have become necessary because of last night's and this morning's events.

"There's a lot of high school trouble today," Mike Stern tells him. "We've got Buder, Clines, Sterba and Nancy Hicks out at various schools covering fighting between blacks and whites."

"Tell the picture desk to get photographers to those schools," Gelb says, "and now let's figure out who's going to write all this."

They decide to wait and see how the story develops. One school may provide the lead, in which case the reporter covering it will write the story, incorporating into it details of what went on at the other schools from memos furnished him by reporters on the spot.

Siegel shows Gelb a story written by Charles Grutzner, the staff expert on the doings and misdoings of the Mafia. Grutzner had tapped his sources inside and outside the organization and had come up with an exclusive about a Mafia front man now in Switzerland. It is scheduled to run tomorrow. "We've got to be careful on this," Gelb warns. "I'll talk to Ed Smith [a Times attorney] to clear it for libel."

"This Peter Kihss piece on the change in the condition of urban Negroes is ready to go," says Siegel, whose principal desk function is to work with reporters on takeouts rather than spot news. Kihss and Homer Bigart, sensitive, zealously thorough and competent men, are the front line of general assignment reporters, the kind every editor wishes he had more of.

"That story's page 1," says Gelb, voicing the ambition of all editors to get as many of their stories as possible on the front page.

"We've got a man covering Councilman Robert Low, who has issued a statement attacking Mayor Lindsay," Alden reports.

"He has the best press agent of the pack," Gelb comments. "Let's not do a story on him every day. Let's do a wrap-up today on all the Democratic candidates for Mayor."

Gelb pulls from his pockets bits and scraps of paper and clippings. "Let's check on vandals in Penn Station," he suggests. Alden makes a note on the assignment schedule.

Gelb reads from a clipping that says Columbia has abandoned its gym project, one of the causes of the University's riots last spring. "How's she going to get a gym? Who's going to replace the trees already cut down to make way for the gym?" Peter Millones, one of the few reporters on the floor at this hour, is summoned by the loud-speaker to the conference and sent out to find the answers.

At his newsroom desk hard by the foreign, national and metropolitan editors, Abe Rosenthal is flipping through agency copy, clueing himself in on the news. Rosenthal had been a brilliant foreign correspondent and a driving and imaginative metropolitan editor before he became, at forty-seven, associate managing editor. He outranks all newsroom editors except James Reston and Clifton Daniel, neither of whom concerns himself primarily with the day-by-day news operation. It is Rosenthal who, in conference with the bullpen editors, will determine early this evening the exact play of the principal stories. Now, in midmorning, he stops by the major news desks to see how things are shaping up.

"What's special?" he asks Gelb.

"Confrontation of blacks and whites in schools. We're trying to find out if it's a pattern. We're talking to parents, teachers, students. . . . SDS is moving into the Democratic clubs in the city. . . . Dick Reeves is doing a story on the candidates for Mayor seeking the endorsement of Ted Kennedy."

"Can't we do a Q-head one of these days on why all the Democrats are entering the mayoralty race?" Rosenthal asks.

"They all have a chance," Gelb tells him. "No one seems able to pull the party together, so it's a free-for-all."

Rosenthal wanders over to the foreign and national desks for similar fill-ins from Topping and Roberts. Then he checks the Associated Press wire at his own desk.

There's nothing on the wire that surprises him after the rundowns he's just gotten. At 10:45 there is nothing to indicate that this will be anything but a routine day.

At 10:46 an Associated Press bulletin out of Washington shatters the routine. It says: GENERAL DWIGHT D. EISENHOWER HAS DEVELOPED PNEUMONIA.

· · · · · · 11 a.m.

The former President had been gravely ill for many months, and detailed preparations had been made for handling the story of his death.

At 11 o'clock this morning it appears that today might be the day. A four-page obituary covering the Eisenhower career in text and photographs is in type in the composing room. Proofs have been pulled and the page forms stored in a composing-room rack against the day when they will be pulled out for insertion in the paper.

Preparing advance obituaries of distinguished people is a common newspaper practice. Should the subject die close to deadline, it would be impossible to write a fair and balanced appraisal, let alone the story of a crowded life, in the haste of making an edition. So the sketch, with side stories to accompany it and photographs to illustrate it, is prepared beforehand and the pages are made up. All that needs to be done at the moment of death is to affix a news lead. This makes it possible to place the person before the reader in the terms, and with the space, that he deserves.

A few minutes after the bulletin comes in announcing Eisenhower's critical condition, proofs of the four-page obituary are on Rosenthal's desk and on the national news desk, which will be responsible for its final editing and updating. Also in type, with proofs on the editors' desks, is an abbreviated obituary that runs only two columns. This has been prepared against the possibility that Eisenhower might die very late at night, too late to allow time to halt the presses for insertion of the four pages and still meet production and distribution schedules. In that event, the longer obituary will be held over and run in all editions the following day.

Reston stops at Rosenthal's desk to ask if the Eisenhower obit is in order. Rosenthal assures him that it is. They enter the managing editor's office, where every morning at 11:30 the top editors get together to bat around ideas for future stories. This is a kind of informal think-tank session, a chance, before the day's pressures bear down too heavily, to leisurely swap opinions that have sprung from today's papers. Out of the exchange generally emerge leads worth investigating and developing. The talk hops around the news, ranges from discussion of great issues to, for example, a suggestion that a reporter be assigned to follow up a two-inch "I don't want to be President" ad that someone had spotted in the paper.

Seated around the long oblong table in the managing editor's office at the southwest corner of the newsroom are Topping, Roberts and Gelb and the three assistant managing editors—Theodore M. Bernstein, Harrison E. Salisbury and Emanuel R. Freedman. These three, equal in rank, have separate duties. Bernstein concentrates on the play of major stories; Salisbury, on the development of special projects; Freedman, on personnel matters.

"I have a terrible feeling that this is the old soldier's last stand," Reston says as he joins his colleagues at the table. "I think there's a great human story in this man's fight, bouncing back from one heart attack after another."

This sets off a chain of ideas. Someone suggests a medical story: Is it possible to keep a man alive with intensive care and tremendous concentration of medical talent? Someone else points out that Eisenhower's doctors have said it's his will to live that has pulled him through.

They decide to ask the Washington bureau to assign a reporter to talk with Eisenhower's doctors to find out if there is
something philosophical in his long struggle for survival. If he
does not die today, this medical history will be played promi-
nently in tomorrow's paper. If he does die, that can wait; the
first imperative is to put the man in historical perspective as
has been done in the prepared obituary.

The talk turns from Eisenhower. Harrison Salisbury mentions a story in this morning's *Wall Street Journal* speculating
on the outcome of the current Congressional investigation of
tax-free Foundations. Reston suggests the possibility of a story
every Monday morning on a big issue that is coming up before the Congress, "a really good analytical story on where it
stands, what the issues are."

Rosenthal breaks in: "I think the idea of examining an issue
that is confronting the legislature or the White House or any
branch of Government is a good one, and that's theoretically
what we should be doing as these issues go along. I wonder,
though, if we do this on an automatic Monday basis whether
we won't find ourselves consuming space simply because it is
scheduled for a Monday. And also whether we will not be delaying stories that we should have before Monday."

It would be a rare week, Reston thinks, when there
wouldn't be something for Monday if it were planned ahead.
Rosenthal holds for breaking into a running story and round-
ing it up "when it should be done," not by day of week. They
agree to wait until Max Frankel, Washington bureau chief, returns from the Nixon tour and get his views.

They touch briefly on the story in today's Times covering
the Congressional hearing on Foundation money. Arthur
Ochs Sulzberger, the publisher, who sits in on these morning
meetings when his schedule permits, wonders why the Times
story failed to mention how much money goes into educa-
tional institutions from Foundation sources. Reston tells
him that's the kind of question so simple that a re-

porter tends to forget it—the kind of thing that would be included, for example, in a Monday morning roundup about the flow of Foundation money to universities.

Emanuel Freedman makes the point that the New York *Daily News* this morning led with something that wasn't even mentioned in The Times story: John D. Rockefeller III's testimony that he doesn't have to pay income tax because he gives all his income away, but that for some years he has voluntarily paid 5 to 10 per cent of his income in taxes.

"And everybody else pays 50 per cent," Rosenthal mutters. "That's an interesting point, that he contributes so much to philanthropy that he doesn't have to pay any tax." Rosenthal makes a note to ask the Washington bureau why it wasn't included in the Times story.

Topping brings up an example of a problem that constantly plagues newspaper editors: the pitfalls that lie in deciding, on deadline, whether to rely on the judgment of your own correspondents at a scene when that judgment is at variance with news service reports.

"The Washington Post's lead this morning on the Nixon reception in Rome," Topping says, "went heavily on anti-Nixon rioting and you could see that the writing was done in the office in Washington from agency dispatches. It was faulty. The assumptions were wrong. Our own reporting by correspondents on the scene explained the motivation of the rioters as distinct from the Nixon visit. It was very good balance. We didn't minimize the extent of the rioting or the significance of it, but we made the proper distinctions and showed the proper relationships, and I thought it rather an interesting example of a technological problem."

Rosenthal had been in Washington yesterday to attend a luncheon in the Washington bureau. The bureau, which can seat fourteen at its dining room table, holds a luncheon a couple of times a month at which an important Government official is the guest of honor. The other guests are usually an editor or two from New York and bureau reporters whose news beats relate to the Government official's field of interest. The talk is informal and off the record. It is a chance to introduce staff members to leading political figures, and vice versa, and to exchange background information that is mutually beneficial. Yesterday's guest had been Secretary of Defense Melvin R. Laird, six weeks in office in the new Nixon Administration.

Rosenthal gives his colleagues a rundown of the luncheon conversation but cautions them that it was all off the record.

The talk turns to issues close to home—hunger in New York, the Negro migration to the suburbs, the movement back to the city of corporate headquarters that fled New York for the suburbs only to find it impossible to operate outside the marketplace.

When the meeting breaks up, the foreign, national and metropolitan editors return to their desks to work out assignments that will ultimately convert many of the ideas batted around the conference table into stories.

• • •

Five thousand miles away in Cairo, C. L. Sulzberger, editorial page columnist, has scored a journalistic coup: an exclusive interview with President Gamal Abdel Nasser of the United Arab Republic, the chief spokesman for the Arab countries. At 11:04, a cable from Sulzberger advises the New York office: AM NOW TRANSMITTING NASSER INTERVIEW PLUS QUESTION AND ANSWER TRANSCRIPT FOR RELEASE SUNDAY, MARCH TWO. Q & A TRANSCRIPT RUNS APPROXIMATELY 3,000 WORDS. NEWS STORY IS ESTIMATED 1,250 WORDS. ALSO TRANSMITTING RADIO PHOTOGRAPHS OF NASSER TALKING WITH ME. CAN EASILY UNDERSTAND YOU MAY WISH CUT QUESTION AND ANSWER TRANSCRIPT BUT APPRECIATE GREAT CARE IN EXCISIONS BECAUSE OF OBVIOUS POLITICAL CONNOTATIONS.

The man on 43d Street to whom this message is of the most

immediate concern is Rob Roy Buckingham, head of The New York Times News Service, which transmits the Times news report to 300 client newspapers and news magazines around the world. Buckingham knows that the Nasser interview will have its most important impact in Europe and the Middle East, where inflammatory Arab-Israeli relations are of most immediate concern, and he had already alerted subscribers in those areas to be on the watch for it. He also knows that the key to getting the mass of material printed rests on delivering it as early as possible to allow foreign-language newspapers time to translate it. So immediately on receipt of Sulzberger's cable that copy is on the way, the News Service clears its decks for transmission of the interview on a "Sunday embargoed" basis (not to be printed, that is, until Sunday, March 2).

Sulzberger had informed Reston in advance that his interview with Nasser would take place on Wednesday, February 26. Reston and Topping decided to schedule it for March 2 in order to give Sulzberger time to clear with Nasser whatever ambiguities might arise during their talk and to give New York time to edit it and process it for publication.

Sulzberger had known Nasser about fifteen years and had seen him many times. A year earlier he had had an appointment with him; but on the day it was to be held a massive Israeli attack on a town in Jordan raised the alarming possibility of a new war, and Nasser dashed off to his desert military headquarters. Sulzberger had been obliged to leave the country without seeing him. The February 26 interview was, in effect, a year-delayed raincheck.

The difficulties of transmitting the interview from Egypt were well known to Sulzberger. It was far too long an accumulation of words for telephone dictation, which, with interruptions, could take many hours. And cable was uncertain because of possible censorship. Besides, he had to arrange for a verbatim transcript of the talk if he were to provide the question-and-answer text that Reston had requested. So he had taken his secretary, Susan Sevray, with him from his office in Paris. She took down in shorthand the entire two-hour interview in Nasser's home. Afterward, in a hotel room, Susan typed out the lengthy question-and-answer text, and Sulzberger went over it, checking it against his own notes. Then he sent it to Nasser by special messenger to be checked for accuracy. The text out of the way, Sulzberger wrote his story of the interview. The text was returned without a single word changed.

The only efficient way of transmitting the material to New York, Sulzberger decided, was from Paris. So Susan had flown back to Paris today, reaching there in midafternoon, a couple of hours after the arrival of President Nixon. She reached The Times's bureau in time to clear the copy to New York before the wire room faced the avalanche of Nixon copy later in the evening.

It is rare for C. L. Sulzberger's by-line to appear on the news pages of The Times. His three-day-a-week column on foreign affairs is an editorial-page feature, as are the columns of Reston and Wicker, who comment primarily on national affairs, and Russell Baker, whose "Observer" column satirizes all kinds of affairs. These columns represent the views of the writers and may disagree wholly with the newspaper's opinions as expressed in its editorials in adjoining columns.

Times editorials reflect the thinking of John Oakes, editorial-page editor, and his eleven-man editorial board. These men, and the publisher, forty-three-year-old Arthur Ochs Sulzberger—who bears final responsibility for what The Times says—believe that the function of an editorial is to provide constructive criticism of news developments and present a point of view on significant controversial issues. They do not want readers left in doubt as to where The Times stands on any major subject.

As a result, Times editorials frequently enrage certain

groups—it may be the liquor industry today, the cigarette manufacturers yesterday, the radicals or stand-patters on the campuses tomorrow. Mr. Oakes's laconic reaction to these manifestations of displeasure is: "Write a letter to the editor" —and the readers do, to the tune of 30,000 a year.

Oakes, whose jurisdiction extends over the "Letters to the Editor" column, sees this feature of the editorial page as a forum for the exchange of informed views, a vehicle for serious discussion of public issues. The number of letters published on an issue generally reflects the proportion of pro and con mail received; but on steamingly controversial subjects on which The Times has taken a strong stand, Oakes believes it is important to give louder voice to positions opposed to the Times's editorial policy.

Each member of the editorial board has certain areas in which he is particularly well fitted to comment by reason of his experience and background, and to which he devotes the greater part of his attention. But any board member may be, and frequently is, asked to write on a subject that does not fall into any of the recognized categories. No writer is asked to write anything with which he does not agree.

Members of the board range far and wide to explore the fields they cover. Today, James P. Brown is in Lebanon, freshening up on the Middle East. William Shannon, whose specialty is national affairs, writes out of Washington, where he maintains live contact with Government officials.

Though each editorial writer works out of a private office, with easy access to The Times's library and its 40,000 reference volumes, there is no ivory-tower atmosphere on the editorial floor. Leaders in almost every field of activity find their way to the tenth floor of the 43d Street plant to take issue with something The Times has said, or applaud its comments, or enlist its support.

This morning, in the absence of Oakes (who is hospitalized with hepatitis), A. H. Raskin, the assistant editorial page editor, is talking in his office with Assemblyman Stanley Steingut, leader of the Democratic minority in the New York State Assembly. Mr. Steingut has been less than flattered at the editorial page's description of him as "boss of the hack-ridden Brooklyn machine" exemplifying all the weaknesses that had caused the Democrats to lose every recent city and state election. He had signified his desire to come in and try to persuade The Times's editors that he was something better than a "knock-about, shopworn county leader," one of the descriptions the editorial had applied.

Two of the board's specialists on state and local politics, Frank S. Adams and John A. Hamilton, are sitting in on the session in Raskin's office. Mr. Steingut emphasizes that he loves The Times even if it does not love him. He is assured in turn that The Times has neither enemies nor friends in public life; that its editors seek to assess without malice each development on the political front, praising those it considers constructive and lambasting those it does not. The meeting breaks up on a friendly note. It's a draw.

· · · · noon

It's far too early to know specifically how tomorrow's paper will shape up. But it's time for each desk to prepare a preliminary schedule of the stories which, as things now stand, will be forthcoming tonight. These early listings serve as a guide to Rosenthal and the news editors who will lay out the first edition six hours from now.

Because it is already late in the day for correspondents abroad, the foreign desk has the clearest picture of what its stories will be. Tanner and Frankel have informed the desk how the Nixon story will be handled from Paris. Terry Smith, before he turned in for the night in Vietnam, cabled the desk a summary of the stories that had already been filed. The summary would reach New York without delay, while the copy might be held up in transmission. Smith had cabled the gist of his 750-word story: ENEMY SHELLS ABOUT THIRTY TARGETS AROUND COUNTRY WHILE U.S. INFANTRYMEN FIGHT DAY LONG BATTLE WITHIN SIX MILES OF SAIGON; and of Charles Mohr's 700 words: INGENIOUS WEAPONS SAVE AMERICAN LIVES DURING OFFENSIVE.

From Rome, Bureau Chief Robert Doty cables that his wrap-up of Nixon's talks with Italian leaders will run 700 words and will stress Italian satisfaction with Nixon's pledge

81

of consultations. He makes a plea for space: HOPE ROOM FOR SIZEABLE CHUNK OF THIS CAN BE FOUND SINCE ITALY, SQUEEZED BETWEEN MORE DRA-MATIC BERLIN AND FRENCH STORIES, HAS HAD THUS FAR ONLY BLACK EYE OF YESTERNIGHT'S FRONT PAGED DISORDERS.

From Berlin, David Binder informs the desk: THERE IS A LOT OF MOVEMENT ON THE BERLIN CONFRONTA-TION TODAY, ALL IN THE DIRECTION OF HARDEN-ING POSITIONS. He outlines the specific occurrences of the day, then adds: I HOPE TO COVER THIS IN ABOUT 900 WORDS, APPRECIATING YOUR SPACE PROBLEM BUT ALSO IN KNOWLEDGE THAT FATIGUE MAKES COR-RESPONDENTS MORE PROLIX. THERE WILL PROBA-BLY BE LATER DEVELOPMENTS, SOME OF WHICH MIGHT POSSIBLY SUPERSEDE PRESENT LIST AND WILL HANDLE APPROPRIATELY.

A cable from Drew Middleton from Brussels, where he is covering a meeting of the North American Treaty Organiza-tion's Nuclear Planning Group, advises: SENDING NEW LEAD AND INSERTS NUCLEAR. APOLOGIZE FOR LENGTH OF LATTER BUT THESE ARE COMPLI-CATED SUBJECTS THAT HAVE TO BE SPELLED OUT TO MAKE SENSE—TO ME ANYHOW.

. . .

A few feet from the foreign desk the national editor and his assistants are taking phone calls from staff men around the country. Lawrence Davies, San Francisco bureau chief, whose beat extends north to Alaska and west to Hawaii, calls in with the cheery news that the sun is trying to shine after a miser-able rainy winter but otherwise, at 9 A.M., prospects for much news that day from San Francisco are not bright. Before he called New York, Davies had checked with Times stringers at San Francisco State College and at the University of Califor-nia at Berkeley to learn that on those frequently erupting campuses all was relatively quiet. Davies's colleague in San Francisco, Wallace Turner, will have no story today. He is working on a comprehensive study of the draft that will keep him busy several weeks.

This is the type of in-depth story that occupies most of the time of regional correspondents. They are concerned not so much with spot news as with national trends and currents. They frequently spend several weeks researching and writing a single takeout, though they are always available, should a big story break in their area, to drop everything and hurry to it.

There will be other news from California tonight. In Los Angeles the trial of Sirhan Bishara Sirhan for the murder of Senator Robert Kennedy is in its tenth week; and in Coronado the Navy court of inquiry investigating the capture by North Korea of the intelligence ship *Pueblo* is in its fifth week. Both these running stories are being covered by staffers sent out from New York rather than by regularly based California correspondents. The editors prefer to keep regional reporters available for area-oriented news rather than tie them down on continuing stories.

The time difference between New York and the West Coast works against reporters on a breaking story. In order to make the first edition, they must file by midafternoon, frequently before the day's events are completed, and send inserts or new leads for later editions.

Bernard Weinraub, the reporter assigned to the *Pueblo* hearing, has gotten an early morning briefing from the Navy public affairs officer, and by noon New York time (it is three hours earlier in California), he is able to call Irv Horowitz on the national desk and tell him: "The same thing today. More crewmen are talking about the detention period. I'll start filing at the luncheon break."

In Los Angeles, Douglas Robinson and Lacey Fosburgh, the two reporters on the Sirhan trial, meet for breakfast in the Ambassador Hotel coffee shop and bemoan the fact that every

day it becomes a little harder to pick a good lead from the
verbal outpourings of the witnesses. Today's testimony, they
agree, promises to be dull, filled with depressing accounts of
life in Jerusalem for the Arabs in 1948. They are joined at
breakfast by Emile Zola Berman, one of Sirhan's defense lawyers, who tears some of the gloom from the day by announcing: "Our client is getting agitated . . . he may blow today."
The reporters press for details, but the attorney clams up. Before he enters the courtroom at 9 A.M., Robinson calls Horowitz. "More defense witnesses today," he says laconically,
though he is a little more hopeful about a good story than he
had been. He will start to write after the noon recess, and
Miss Fosburgh will cover the afternoon session and notify him
if anything newsworthy develops. Only one reporter from a
newspaper is permitted in the heavily guarded courtroom at a
time.

Gene Roberts takes a call from Roy Reed in Austin, Texas,
where he is trying to piece together a story on Lyndon Johnson, who has avoided the press since he left Washington six
weeks earlier. Reed has been in Austin three days, and he still
has no prospect of an interview with the former President.
He's the only out-of-town reporter in the city. He tells Roberts
how lonely the place is. He mentions that his hotel, the Driskill, which used to be the center of activity for press and staff
when President Johnson visited the LBJ ranch, is now almost
deserted and is about to be torn down because it is losing
money. Roberts reacts quickly. "While you're waiting around
for an interview," he says, "give us a story on the decline and
fall of Austin as a world capital." Reed cheers up, hangs up
and sets to work.

He had noticed when he arrived at the Driskill that someone had dropped cigarette ashes in the hollows of the ears of
an LBJ bust in the lobby. He decides to use that inconsequential, yet revealing, fact as the tag line of his story because it
describes so vividly the fallen state of Austin. He goes down

to the lobby to make sure the ashes are still there. They are. (When his story reached New York, it was held for several days before it was published. This posed a knotty little problem for Reed. Every afternoon he checked Lyndon's ears to make sure the ashes were still there. If he had found them cleaned out, which he did not, he would have had to revise the ending of his story. Such are the small details that can plague a reporter.)

Shortly after noon the Washington bureau sends New York by teletype a list of its stories to be incorporated in the national desk's schedule. The list includes: "Ike—(Belair)—Gen. Eisenhower develops pneumonia."

Felix Belair, Jr., a veteran Washington correspondent, is a close friend of Eisenhower's. The two men had gotten to know each other while Eisenhower was President and Belair was White House correspondent for The Times. After he left office, Eisenhower frequently called Belair to his home in Gettysburg to talk to him as a friend and to give him tips that led to exclusive stories. Around Washington, Belair is known as the press corps's "Number One Ikeologist."

This morning Belair had attended a 10 o'clock press conference on the formation by a private organization of an Overseas Development Council to promote economic development of underdeveloped nations. When he reached the bureau about 11:30 and reported to David Jones on the news desk that there seemed to be a pretty good story in the Development Council, Jones told him that Eisenhower had developed pneumonia. Belair had written the two-column abbreviated obituary several months earlier, after Eisenhower's seventh heart attack, and had updated it several times since. He knows the full-length four-page obit is also in good shape. So he sits down at his desk and bats out a story on the Development Council. After lunch he will get on the phone to his private medical sources on Eisenhower.

Each desk prepares its schedule of prospective stories.

Every story is marked with an identifying slug, or code description, that will stay with it as it is written, edited, processed in the composing room and placed in the page form. The schedule also carries the name of the reporter who will write the story and a terse summary of what it is about.

Today's metropolitan desk schedule lists twenty-five possible stories, including:

Dems—Reeves—Democratic Mayoral candidates seeking advice and endorsement of Sen. [Edward] Kennedy.

Census—Kihss—Census study shows both progress and fallbacks for Negroes in New York.

Mafia—Grutzner—Mafia money man in Switzerland expedites investments in legitimate businesses.

High—Buder—Interracial fighting at high schools, with Sterba at Jefferson, Clines at Lane, Buder at Jackson, Johnston at Irving.

Regents—Albany bureau—State Board of Regents meeting and news conference.

There are eighteen potential stories on the national desk schedule, among them:

Taxes—Shanahan—Hearings resume on Foundation reforms.

Intelsat—Finney—Russian position in communications satellite negotiations.

Sirhan—Robinson—Defense continues its case.

Pueblo—Weinraub—More crewmen tell about their captivity.

Shaw—Waldron—Case may go to jury late today.

Leak—Blair—Secretary Hickel testifying before Senate committee on air and water pollution.

The foreign desk schedule still looks as it did when Topping came in a couple of hours earlier: "Nixon," "Berlin," "Vietnam," "Nuclear," "Eshkol," etc.

Lewis Jordan, the news editor, who determines space allotments for each news category, will scan these listings when he reaches the office in early afternoon. They will guide him in determining how many columns of tomorrow's paper to assign to local, national and foreign news.

· · ·

Clive Barnes, the drama and dance critic, has had a busy morning. He had worked at his home until almost 4 A.M., and at 8:30 he was up—shaved, showered and doing the Royal Canadian Air Force Exercises. He took a flurry of telephone calls over breakfast coffee—from Anthony Bliss, who wanted to discuss the possibility of building a permanent dance theater in New York; from Bernhard Leitner, a friend who is a Viennese architect and wanted to discuss new theaters being planned for Broadway. By midmorning he has reached the cultural news department, an adjunct of the third-floor newsroom. He checks the mail. He has a letter from a judge in Detroit who praises him to the skies (in itself a rarity). It is balanced by a letter from a lady in the Middle West who complains bitterly about his review of the Theater of the Deaf, which she considered too harsh. There's a letter from a homosexual student at Northwestern University thanking him for suggesting in his appraisal of *The Boys in the Band* that not all homosexuals are unhappy. He takes a phone call from a gentleman asking him to see his free play, off-off-off Broadway. He explains that he cannot see every play in New York and as a general rule goes only to professional performances. A press agent of an off-Broadway play, *Spitting Image,* calls to ask whether he wants to go to a press preview or to the first night. He says he'll be there the first night; he has dance performances to see on the earlier date. He plows through the mail—thirty to forty pieces—chiefly circulars, fliers, releases and the like.

· · ·

Vartanig Vartan, casing New York's financial district for market trends, glances up at the cold, leaden sky and thinks: "This is bear-market weather." He has already caught the early trend of the market through calls to a couple of brokers. The market is up a little, he learns, but conglomerate issues, as he suspected, are on the easy side because of the statement by the president of the New York Stock Exchange that the Big Board is considering delisting the shares of two conglomerate companies.

He drops in, as he does every morning, on several brokerage houses. At Bache & Company, he talks to salesmen, analysts, partners and officials, and even customers, or tape watchers, in the board room. He mingles among the clients and listens unobtrusively to their comments. This is one way of getting the public's sentiment about the market. At Walston & Co. he asks a secretary, "How's the market?" She replies, "We're up today, thank goodness." On the ground floor of Walston's offices he looks over the largest board room in Wall Street. About 150 tape watchers are leaning over the railing at the back of the room or standing against the rear wall. He knows that the market is up by looking at the faces of the crowd; the faces are a bit cheerier than usual today. He steps into the office of Eldon A. Grim, Walston's senior vice-president. They talk about the market this morning; blue chips are up a bit, but the big news is obviously going to be the weakness in conglomerates. He and Grim have an early lunch in the New York Stock Exchange's Luncheon Club at 14 Wall Street.

● ● ●

In Europe, Africa and the Middle East, evening is closing in. Correspondents are at their typewriters. Some have already finished writing and are sending their stories, by telephone and telex, to the London bureau, from which they will be carried by cable across the Atlantic into the 43rd Street wire room.

It is 7 P.M. in Jerusalem, and James Feron is ready to write his piece about Premier Levi Eshkol's funeral. He ponders his lead. Once he decides what he wants to say, and constructs a lead offering the reader that impression, the rest of the story, he knows, will come easy. In the death of Eshkol he sees the passing of an era; that's the impression he wants to convey. He taps out:

"Levi Eshkol was buried today with the nation's founders atop Mt. Herzl after a simple, but moving, state funeral in the Israel capital."

It pleases him. It gives the picture he wants. (The fact that it was changed slightly by the copydesk in New York to read: "Levi Eshkol was buried with Israel's founders atop Mount Herzl today after a simple and moving state funeral" didn't bother him. He believes there are many ways to reach the reader, and if the copyreader thinks he has a better way, that's fine with Feron. Many reporters do not have such a benign attitude toward the copydesk. Certain copyreaders, they readily admit, improve and embellish the stories they handle but, traditionally, reporters are inclined to feel that every copydesk alteration—except for a factual or grammatical error—is for the worse.)

Feron continues at the typewriter:

"The Premier, who died Wednesday at the age of 73, was laid to rest next to Yosef Sprinzak, whose personal inspiration drew Mr. Eshkol here five decades ago." (The copydesk changed this sentence to read: "The grave of the Premier, who died of a heart attack Wednesday at the age of 73, is next to that of Yosef Sprinzak, whose personal inspiration drew Mr. Eshkol here five decades ago." Feron thought the change good. It removed "laid to rest," which he hadn't liked much anyway, and it added the information that Eshkol died of a heart attack.)

The next three paragraphs, which completed the point he wanted to make, were printed as he wrote them, except for one or two word changes:

"A memorial stone atop the Sprinzak grave refers to him as

the first speaker of the Knesset (Parliament), but it was as a Zionist leader in Russia of the early 1900's that Mr. Eshkol cherished him.

"Sprinzak spoke to young Levi Shkolnik, as he was then called, of the work that was being done in Palestine, of the land settlement and of the hopes to build a Jewish nation.

"This morning, under a warm sun, the Russian settler who was to become that nation's leader was carried to his final rest after having lain in state since yesterday morning."

By beginning the story this way, Feron was trying to convey the span of Jewish settlement that Eshkol represented and his role in the nation he helped build. It was a lengthy bypass —all the business about Sprinzak—but it seemed important to put Eshkol into some sort of manageable framework for the reader.

With the scene set, the story flowed quickly from his typewriter.

. . .

In Bucharest, Tad Szulc is at the typewriter, too. He flips through the notes he scribbled during the marathon 102-minute campaign speech by President Nicholae Ceausescu. His notes indicate that the speech was interrupted every five minutes by formal applause but that the applause was spontaneous and enthusiastic every time Ceausescu promised that, if re-elected, Rumania would maintain its independence of Soviet leadership. This, it seemed to Szulc, was the gist of the seemingly endless speech. He wrote:

"President Nicholae Ceausescu asked Rumanians today to turn the parliamentary elections next Sunday into a vote of confidence for his Government's increasingly independent foreign policies." Then he described the "applauding audience," the "repeated standing ovations" as Ceausescu provided examples of these independent policies.

. . .

In London, Anthony Lewis gets out the material he has accumulated for the profile he is going to write on John Freeman, the new British Ambassador to the United States. Freeman will leave for his new post within a day or so, and the profile will run as a "Man in the News" the day after he takes up his duties in Washington.

A few days earlier, while Tom Wicker was in London during the Nixon visit, Lewis and Wicker had lunched with Freeman. Lewis recalls a remark Freeman made at the luncheon that, he thought, revealed a great deal about the man. But he can't recollect it fully enough to quote it. So he telephones Wicker, now in Paris, to see if he remembers the gist of the remark. Wicker does.

Lewis decides to begin his profile with it. He writes:

"At lunch recently with John Freeman, a visiting American remarked that students today seemed to see conspiracy everywhere; they had no idea of life's accidental quality, its tragedy and comedy. 'I think that is the definition of maturity,' Mr. Freeman replied, 'when one passes from the conspiracy theory to the sense of tragicomedy.'

"The remark may help to clear away any lingering misconceptions about a complex person of whom Americans will be seeing a good deal. . . ."

·····1 p.m.

As the New York newsroom empties for lunch, the London bureau approaches the peak of its day's activity. It is 7 P.M., and editors, deskmen and wire-room operators move into high gear.

Gloria Emerson has reported to Lewis that the Parliament debate on the Sunday blue laws, which she attended this morning, was not very funny. But when she described it to him, he told her it sounded funnier than she thought; she should go ahead and write it. (She may have been right, Lewis conceded later. The story was cut to a short in New York.) First, though, Miss Emerson finishes a story she is writing for the women's page on Queen Elizabeth's mail. That done, she cables Joan Whitman, assistant women's news editor in New York: FILING TODAY STORY ON MAIL SENT TO QUEEN IN BUCKINGHAM PALACE. MUCH HAMPERED BY REFUSAL OF STAFF TO LET ME SEE LETTERS, ESPECIALLY FROM AMERICANS BUT THAT'S THE WAY THE CRUMPET CRUMBLES. ARE YOU INTERESTED IN INTERVIEW WITH MOTHER OF GINGER ROGERS WHO SAID SOME HORRIFIC THINGS ON BBC INTERVIEW? GINGER HERE IN "AUNTIE MAME."

Mrs. Whitman replies "No" on Ginger's mother.

John Lee, who has a dossier on the construction problems that have delayed delivery of Cunard's new luxury liner, the *Queen Elizabeth II*, learns that the government is about to release its report on the liner's turbine troubles. He gets out his Cunard folder, calls the Ministry of Technology for a highly technical discussion of turbines and, after cabling New York that he will file a story indicating that the turbine problem is apparently solved, begins to write. At an adjoining desk, Alvin Shuster is finishing his story on the new government regulations about to be imposed on British gambling casinos.

The flow through the bureau's wire room approaches flood tide as copy headed for New York pours in by telephone and telex, and cables between the home office and correspondents around the world chatter through for relay.

Telex printers tap out Moshe Brilliant's story from Tel Aviv on the Suez Canal flare-up, and Feron's story from Jerusalem on the Eshkol funeral. Telex copy comes into the London wire room on tape and is relayed to New York without repunching. But London deskmen must read the print-out to make sure the copy is not garbled. Tonight, for example, Larry Fellows's story about the rains in Kenya has come in backward. Joe Frayman, the bureau's senior deskman, calls Cable & Wireless, the commercial cable company over whose lines the copy was sent from Nairobi, to ask that they check the original copy and notify him exactly how it should read.

Drew Middleton telephones from Brussels and dictates into a recording machine revisions of his European nuclear story. David Binder telephones from Berlin and dictates his story on Communist threats over the West German elections. Henry Kamm calls from Moscow and schedules two stories—one by him on culture in the Ukraine; the other by his associate, Bernard Gwertzman, about the shortages of consumer goods in Russia. The stories themselves will be telephoned later for relay to New York.

Messages and queries leap back and forth across the Atlantic, pausing in the London wire room for relay. Reston cables C. L. Sulzberger: SINCERE THANKS AND ADMIRA- TION FOR THE INTERESTING INTERVIEW WITH NAS- SER. The message is forwarded to Sulzberger, who is still in Cairo. Tad Szulc telephones from Bucharest to schedule his story on Ceausescu and advise Topping: PLAN TO FILE EARLY SATURDAY FOR SUNDAY A FEATURE ON MY BALKAN RAILROAD MEANDERINGS OF THIS WEEK. IT WILL HAVE UNPRONOUNCEABLE DATE- LINE.

Max Frankel phones Lewis from Paris to talk about the Nixon trip. He is calling from the press headquarters set up for reporters in the Hotel Georges Cinq. Frankel is working on a piece for Sunday's "Week in Review" section in which he will analyze the accomplishments of the trip, and he wants to kick some thoughts around with Lewis, particularly about the impact of the London stopover.

Bob Semple, meanwhile, faced with the problem of writ- ing today's news story on the trip, is prowling the hotel corri- dors, trying to pry from the President's spokesmen something of substance that may have emerged from Nixon's two-hour private talk with de Gaulle this afternoon.

Nixon has been invisible to the press since he arrived in Paris. After his talks with de Gaulle, he returned to his own quarters at the Quai D'Orsay, conferred with Henry A. Kissin- ger, his adviser on national security affairs, and with Secretary of State William P. Rogers, and transacted some White House business. Semple knows that the President's mind is preoccu- pied by de Gaulle and the Middle East. He also knows that Nixon used some of his free time this afternoon to prepare for his talks Sunday morning with Vice President Ky of South Vietnam, who is in Paris representing his country at the peace talks. But what Semple does not have are any details, any hard news for tonight's story.

In the hotel lobby he waylays Robert McCloskey, the State

Department spokesman, and Ronald L. Ziegler, the President's press secretary. They say only that the talks with de Gaulle represented a "full, frank and cordial exchange of views." To Semple this means that Nixon has assured de Gaulle he does not wish to impose his designs on Europe and that the General has begun to believe these assurances. It still leaves him without much hard news. He attends a press briefing by Ziegler. Nothing new. He grabs a quick bite in the hotel's hospitality suite and glances at the clock. It's after 7 P.M. He had better begin to write.

• • •

In New York, Food Editor Craig Claiborne is eating, too. He's a professional eater. Lunch, for him, is not a quick grab to sustain him for the rest of the day's work. Mealtime is when he checks new prospects for his "Guide to Dining Out" listing, a Friday morning feature of the women's page in which he reviews restaurants on a star system, from four stars down to none.

Today, Claiborne and his friend Pierre Franey, the chef who made New York's Le Pavillon the most illustrious French restaurant in America, are testing a new restaurant, La Fondue, on East 55th Street. It specializes, as the name implies, in cheeses and cheese dishes.

The restaurant has not yet acquired a liquor license, so it has no bar. That means no wine. Unthinkable. Claiborne stops by a liquor store and buys a bottle of Meursault-Charmes 1966, a dry white burgundy.

As usual when he enters a restaurant, he does not identify himself. Whenever he can, he goes incognito and unannounced so that he can sample the food without special preparation and special service. He wants to find it exactly as his readers will find it—same food, same service.

He is a trim, unobtrusive-looking man with a cherubic face. Though he dines professionally at least seven times a week, he keeps trim because he only samples each course. He eats a variety of food but not a lot of any single dish. He seldom cleans his plate.

He likes to dine with at least one companion so that he can taste a wider variety of dishes than he would alone. This noon, for a first course, he orders matjes herring on Boston lettuce leaves garnished with lemon wedges; Franey begins with cheddar cheese soup. For the entrée, Claiborne has a cheese fondue and Franey orders a platter of assorted charcuterie (a fancy French name for cold cuts) and cheeses. They nibble from each other's plates and exchange opinions about each dish.

Claiborne jots down notes in a tiny memo pad, about the size of Melba toast, that he always carries.

"Rather grainy," is his entry on the cheese soufflé. He describes the cheddar cheese soup as "interesting."

They have espresso and pass up dessert. On the way out Claiborne asks for the lunch and dinner menus, as he always does. The tab, which The Times will pick up, comes to $16.10, the wine included.

In his thumbnail review of La Fondue in the "Guide to Dining Out" listing, Claiborne will give it two stars, calling it "longer on inspiration than execution" but still a welcome addition to New York restaurants.

• • •

A few blocks to the south, Philip Dougherty, the advertising columnist, is the luncheon guest of two agency executives at a small, elegant Italian restaurant that's "in" with the Madison Avenue advertising and public relations crowd. As he sips his Scotch old-fashioned, he reflects for a moment on the days when he was a society reporter and his friends all thought "How chic." His lunches then generally consisted of a Swiss cheese sandwich in The Times's cafeteria.

An advertising columnist has much easier access to his news sources than does a general assignment reporter, Dougherty, who has also done a turn on general assignment, muses

as he sips his Italian spinach soup. These fellows in advertising are an excessively friendly bunch—lunches, dinners, cock-
tails. You've got to stay constantly alert to winnow the real
news from the "plants."

Actually, though, he decides as he winds up his lunch with
a chocolate mousse, a reporter's a reporter no matter what his
beat. He still has to do the leg work, ask the questions and
sniff out the real stories.

                                                    • • •

The Times's top editors have joined the publisher for lunch in
his mahogany-paneled dining room on the eleventh floor of
the 43rd Street plant.

The publisher has come from a meeting with his business
executives on a knotty policy problem: Should The Times
continue to accept cigarette advertising in view of the medical
evidence of the perils of smoking? The editorial page, reflecting the publisher's opinion, has long plugged for legislation requiring stronger warnings of health hazards than the small-
type notice on each package. The problem confronting the
publisher and his advisers is not loss of revenue; in the previous year only about 115,000 of the more than 86 million
lines of advertising published in The Times were for cigarettes. It is philosophical. As long as cigarette sales are legal,
can The Times, in good conscience, refuse such advertising
and still be consistent with its tradition of accepting all legitimate comers, barring only the offensive, misleading and un-
trustworthy?

(There was no decision today, but a few months later The
Times announced that it would require health warnings and
disclosure of tar and nicotine content on all cigarette advertising after January 1, 1970. Advertisers, outraged, pulled their
linage from The Times faster than cigarettes turn to ash.)

Before he joins the publisher at lunch, A. H. Raskin, acting
on behalf of John Oakes, his ailing chief, gives Mr. Sulzberger
a rundown of the themes of editorials in preparation. In the

hour before lunch, Raskin has visited the members of the editorial board in their offices to check out what each man is working on and to discuss the general line each editorial will take.

He tells the publisher that Robert Kleiman, the board's expert on Europe and the Far East, is preparing tomorrow's lead editorial: clarification of the "understanding" with Hanoi that accompanied the decision to halt American bombing of North Vietnam. There was no "understanding," the editorial will point out, save the terms under which the United States would resume the bombing. The point is significant, The Times believes, because the notion that the Communists were reneging on an agreement—a notion deliberately fostered by some high Government sources—could lead to United States overreaction that might torpedo the Paris peace talks.

Herbert Mitgang, the editorial board's nonspecialist, who writes about general topics, is putting the cream cheese and lox on an editorial for tomorrow entitled "Mafia Bagels, Yet?" He comments on the intrusion of the Mafia into a wide variety of legitimate businesses, including Kosher frankfurters and bagels. Mitgang's editorial will warn that neither New York nor the country can afford conglomerates in crime.

Graham Hovey, the board's expert on African affairs, who has recently returned from a fact-finding visit to Africa, has just about completed a gloomy assessment of the Nigerian civil war. This will run under his by-line as a Monday morning editorial-page column. Except for these Monday pieces, editorial writers work in total anonymity.

                                                       • • •

Three or four days a week the publisher has as his luncheon guest a prominent public figure. It may be a Government official, a foreign diplomat, a candidate for office, an important business or financial executive. The luncheons are off the record, and the guests know they can speak freely—though the fact that they're surrounded by newspapermen tends to keep them from saying anything they are anxious to hold secret.

These luncheons are a long-time tradition of Times publishers. Guests have included many of the world's great—kings, queens, heads of foreign governments, Presidential candidates and Presidents emeritus, and one President in office, Lyndon B. Johnson.

Today's guest, though not of that stature, is very much in the news at the moment. He is Congressman James Scheuer, one of the pack of candidates seeking the Democratic nomination for Mayor of New York.

There are fourteen men seated around the long oval dining table set with an Irish linen cloth, gold-banded china and a centerpiece of greenery. Besides the regulars—the chief editors in the news, Sunday and editorial departments—the publisher has asked, as he always does, a few other editors who are particularly involved in the guest's sphere of activity. Today the nonregulars include Frank Adams and John Hamilton of the editorial board, and Metropolitan Editor Arthur Gelb, all of whom are concerned with local politics.

The talk turns on a general discussion of Scheuer's prospects in the mayoralty race. The editors fire questions. What does he consider the city's major problems? What will he do about them if elected? Scheuer, an astute politician, has ready answers. The exchange, as always, is mutually advantageous. The Times men get a chance to meet and question news sources they might not otherwise come into personal contact with, and the guest has a chance to explain his position on issues and to get a sense of the people who direct The Times's news and editorial policies.

· · · · · · 2 p.m.

The first order of business for Lewis Jordan, the 6 foot 4 inch news editor, when he comes in shortly after 2 o'clock is to determine the news hole—the total number of news columns—in tomorrow's paper. He is guided in his judgment by the preliminary schedules of the six news categories— foreign, national, metropolitan, sports, financial and culture —that he finds awaiting him on his desk in the bullpen. (The bullpen, so-called for no apparent reason except that its occupants were once enclosed by a low wooden fence, is a small area of the newsroom where the news editor and his assistants sit.)

Actually, Jordan had a pretty good idea before he came in how tomorrow's paper would shape up. At about noon he had received a call at his home from Eileen Butler, the bullpen secretary, giving him the estimated number of pages in tomorrow's paper and the extra space needs, above the normal allotment, of each desk. She had told him that the national desk needed two columns for the Shaw trial, two for the Sirhan trial, two for the *Pueblo* hearing and, if Eisenhower died, forty columns for his obituary; the foreign desk would need a full page for the Nixon story and three columns for the Eshkol funeral and pictures; the metropolitan desk would like about three columns for stories on school turbulence and four

100

columns for the activities of the State Legislature, which was winding up its session in Albany. She had also given Jordan the advertising department's estimate that tomorrow's paper would be sixty or sixty-four pages.

From this rundown Jordan knew that news would be heavy tonight. He told Miss Butler to inform the advertising department that the news hole would be 200 columns.

The number of pages in the paper is determined by the amount of advertising, but the news content is determined solely by the editors. Each desk has a quota, but the quotas are flexible. They may be cut back or expanded as news dictates. And the editors know that should an important story break between editions, they can avail themselves of their prerogative of ordering advertising stripped from the paper to make room for it.

As Jordan flips through the schedules on his desk, he sees no reason to revise his earlier estimate of 200 columns. His job now is to juggle space requests, which invariably exceed the space available, and try to reduce the total to 200. (The news hole in a Saturday paper is somewhat smaller than on other weekdays because most Government offices, which ordinarily generate a considerable volume of news, close early on Friday.)

· · ·

One floor below the newsroom, a 325-man sales staff, headed by Max Falk, the advertising director, is going after linage to provide the revenue for financing the newspaper's operation. Their efforts bring in more than $100 million a year. A full-page advertisement costs, roughly, $5,500 in a weekday edition, $7,000 on Sunday.

Each of the four main advertising divisions—national, retail, financial and classified—includes dozens of individual classifications covering almost every product and service. Salesmen use the telephone and pound the pavement calling on company and agency executives. Others set out from 43d

Street for selling trips to Europe, South America and the Far East to comb these areas for advertising from governments and industries. Regional salesmen blanket the country, from Boston to San Francisco to Miami.

The fruits of their quest stream into the production office, adjacent to the advertising department, to be prepared for publication. Most advertisements come in the form of copy and artists' layouts—words that must be converted into type in The Times's composing room, illustrations that must be transformed into metal in the photoengraving shop.

The ads scheduled for tomorrow's paper are listed on a master sheet. In early afternoon, Ray Nelan and John Fiala of the publication office transfer them, in exact size, to page dummies, or scratches—sheets of paper ruled into eight columns to simulate a newspaper page. As they place the ads, page by page, Nelan and Fiala are guided by news department requests for "open space"—ad-free areas on specified pages where news can be displayed with attractive layouts.

Nelan and Fiala have a pretty good idea, as they position the ads, which pages will contain what news. They make every effort not to place an ad next to a related news story, but sometimes it is not until after the first edition is printed that they spot a goof and remedy it. Buick, for example, recently ran a big ad announcing that its new models were on display. This showed up in the first edition directly below a news story on the new Buick. To Nelan and Fiala, trained strictly in The Times's policy of absolute separation of news and advertising, this bespoke collusion where no collusion existed. In later editions seven pages separated the ad from the story.

They try just as earnestly to separate competitive advertising. If Lord & Taylor, for instance, is advertising women's shoes, an I. Miller ad will not be placed on the same page. Nor would an ad for Tums be placed in close juxtaposition to a liquor ad. When slip-ups occur, they are usually caught after the first edition. An office classic was a "Drink Great Bear Spring Water" ad that ran through all editions directly above a liquor ad inquiring: "Wouldn't you *rather* drink Four Roses?"

• • •

Copy is beginning to pile up now. In the wire room a battery of forty teleprinters tirelessly punches it out from all over the country, from all over the world. Clerks strip it off the leased wires from the Washington and London bureaus and off the wires of the dozen-odd news agencies that service The Times. The most prolific agency wires are the Associated Press (which runs over 500,000 words a day); the United Press International (about 200,000); Reuters, the British news agency; and Tass, the Soviet agency. Others, such as Dow Jones Financial Service and the United Nations Service, are of a more specific nature.

In the telephone recording room, adjoining the wire room, operators monitor and transcribe another 40,000 words dictated by correspondents throughout the United States, Canada and the Caribbean.

All these words, as they come in, are sorted for the different desks that will handle them. Much is duplication, for on any important event the major wire services and The Times's own correspondents will send stories. The editors use agency copy primarily as a guide and a backstop against the possibility that a reporter's copy may not get in on time. More than 90 per cent of the stories in The Times are "special"; written, that is, by The Times's own staff.

The paper can accommodate only about 150,000 of the almost two million words that cascade in every twenty-four hours, and the appraisal and selection of those words is the essence of the editing of *The New York Times.*

• • •

By 2 o'clock, most of the fourteen seats around the rim of the horseshoe-shaped foreign copydesk are filled. The copydesks comprise one element of the foreign, national and metropolitan desk clusters. The men who handle foreign news come in earlier than other deskmen because the stories they process—from abroad where it's six to thirteen hours later than in New York—come in earlier than national or local stories.

Gerald Gold, assistant foreign news editor, grapples with the copy piled up in front of him. It is his responsibility to prepare the foreign news report for the paper—organize the copy as it comes in, make the final decision on how long each story will run and determine which can be held over for another day. He has reviewed the schedule with Topping and the assistant at his side, Evan Jenkins, who follows through on assignments. That schedule is now on Gold's desk. He checks it against the copy in front of him.

The stories are in from Smith and Mohr in Vietnam (where it is already 3 o'clock tomorrow morning); in also are Binder's story from Berlin, Middleton's from Brussels, Fellows's from Nairobi, Feron's from Jerusalem, Brilliant's from Tel Aviv, Doty's from Rome.

Gold gives each a quick go-through, marks it with the number of words it is to run and passes it to Jack Badiner, the copydesk slot man (the trade term for head of the desk). Badiner skims through it to make sure no major changes are called for. If there are, Gold will cable the writer for a fill-in, and he'd like to reach him before he turns in for the night. It makes for better relations. Correspondents don't relish middle-of-the-night queries from New York.

Badiner passes the story to a copyreader on the rim of his desk who edits it—checks it for accuracy, cuts it down to the space allotted for it, scans it as to construction, good taste and possible libel, and writes the headline.

Though every copyreader is qualified to edit any story that crosses the desk, most of the foreign deskmen—many of whom have served as foreign correspondents—have some background on the stories they handle. As far as possible, they work on copy emanating from the parts of the world with which they are familiar. Their knowledge qualifies them to measure a story's value, to play up what is important and eliminate the trivial.

But equally important is the copyreader's ability to write headlines that fit their space to the fraction of a letter yet tell the story clearly and accurately. Headline writing is a precise art and one of the least appreciated, even in a newspaper office.

Gold flips through the cables from London listing stories still to come. He notes that both Henry Kamm and Bernard Gwertzman will be filing from Moscow; but if it's a heavy night, as it looks to be, their stories can be held over a day. They are features, not hard news.

• • •

In Moscow, it's 10 P.M. Kamm has finished his story on culture in the Ukraine, pegged to his telephone conversation with the Ukrainian culture lady criticized in *Pravda*. Gwertzman has written about the shortage of consumer goods, based on a recent report in the Soviet Parliament about the difficulty of buying teapots. They are on the phone to the London bureau, dictating their stories into a recorder for transmission to New York. That will wind up their day.

Before he goes upstairs to his apartment, Kamm takes a final look at the Tass news ticker running in his office. His eyebrows jump as he reads:

"The Soviet Union has sent a note to East Germany calling for action against alleged West German military recruitment and manufacture of military equipment in West Berlin."

This could mean trouble in the bubbling East-West crisis over the upcoming West German elections.

In New York, Gold's eyebrows rise, too. At 2:15 a United Press bulletin quoting the Tass report reaches his desk.

A flurry of messages pass through the London bureau wire room. Binder signals from Berlin that he will file a new lead on his story slugged "Facedown," based on the Soviet note.

The foreign desk cables Kamm: BINDER WRITING ON SO-
VIET NOTE. WE'D LIKE INTERPRETIVE FROM YOU.

Gold calls the New York office of Tass and learns that the
agency will provide the text of the note. He informs Jordan in
the bullpen that the foreign desk will need an additional column for the text.

Jordan is knocking down space requests, trying to reduce
the requested 225½ columns to the 200 set aside for the news
hole. He subtracts from each desk's request, basing his judgments on what he knows of the news from the preliminary
schedules. At his side, Lawrence Hauck, assistant news editor,
goes through the mounting stacks of incoming bulletins and
copy, tossing over to Jordan whatever he thinks is fodder for
page 1.

As he goes through the copy, Hauck sizes up the tone of
the news with an eye to selecting a "Quotation of the Day" to
run above the "News Summary and Index" on the first page of
the second section. He's on the watch for something significant, yet on the light side, to balance the rather heavy news
that seems to predominate today. He passes over quotations
by people who are constantly in the news (the President, for
example, who makes a speech or a statement almost every day
and could be a constant source of the daily quotation). He
will have to see more copy than is now before him—it will be
5 or 5:30 this afternoon before he definitely picks the
quotation—but he puts aside, for consideration, a summary
sent in by William E. Farrell of the Albany bureau. It says:
"State Education Commissioner announces that high school
girls will be allowed to participate with boys in noncontact
sports in an experimental program to determine whether such
activities are feasible." There might be a good quotation there
when the copy comes in.

Jordan puts out a call for a "Man in the News" prospect.
This daily profile of someone who figures in the news is not

always an obvious choice, since the editors prefer not to use the same individual more than once every two years.

Today is one of those days when the people making page 1 news have been eliminated because they have been profiled too recently. Jordan dials the desk editors on the interoffice phone. "Got a man?" he asks each. They'll look.

Horowitz, on the national desk, calls David Jones in the Washington bureau to see if he has any suggestions. Jones suggests J. Curtis Counts, the new director of the Federal Mediation and Conciliation Service, about whom Jones himself had written a profile which is being held awaiting a news peg. Today's peg, Jones thinks, might be Counts's involvement in trying to settle an American Airlines strike. A few minutes later, though, Jones sends a message to Horowitz: SCRATCH COUNTS PROFILE. HE IS NOT INVOLVED IN AIR STRIKE. Instead, Jones suggests, how about a profile, already in type, on Secretary of Labor George Shultz? To provide a peg for Shultz, Jones tells Horowitz he will ask John Herbers, one of the bureau's urban affairs specialists, to finish a story he has been researching on the changes Shultz wants to make in the Federal Manpower Program.

Herbers is at his desk working on a story about Negro leaders. He reluctantly agrees to drop it and finish the manpower story instead. This means he must get fully educated in a complex program in one afternoon. He gets on the phone to people in various Government agencies; he goes through clips in the bureau's files. He accumulates enough material to begin to write, though as he pounds his typewriter he has the uneasy feeling that there is a lot underneath that would help the story. But time is running out. He puts it together without much sense of satisfaction.

• • •

Sports Editor Jim Roach has asked for twenty-one columns in tomorrow's paper. His desk phone buzzes. Jordan wants to know if there's something special—something he, Jordan, might not know about. No, Roach tells him, just a heavy load of routine events. He ticks them off: basketball, track, skiing, racing, golf, spring training. "Hold it to fifteen," Jordan orders.

The sports department occupies an immense 500 square yards on the newsroom floor. Its fifty-five-man staff includes editors, columnists, reporters, copyreaders and clerical help who keep the calendar of upcoming events. Sports is a self-contained unit, a sort of newspaper within a newspaper. It selects its own pictures, lays out its own pages, has its own make-up editor and copydesk, and gets wire-service copy on all sports—as backstop to staff coverage—from its own battery of teleprinters.

Its two dozen writers' desks are seldom filled. Its reporters are in the field where the action is. Today, five are in semitropical Florida. Joseph Durso is at the Mets' spring training camp in St. Petersburg, George Vecsey is with the Yankees at Fort Lauderdale, and Arthur Daley is shuttling among all the Florida camps for grist for the "Sports of The Times" columns, which he and young Robert Lipsyte take turns writing. Joe Nichols is covering the races at Hialeah, and Lincoln Werden is in Miami with the touring golf pros. Two other reporters have left icy Manhattan for even icier spots: Nelson Bryant, the "Wood, Field and Stream" columnist, is ice fishing in a New Hampshire lake and wondering, as he cuts holes in the snow-covered ice, whether it might not be wiser to cooperate with winter and allow the fish and fishermen some respite; and Michael Strauss is covering the World Cup slalom ski races in a blinding snowstorm at Squaw Valley, California.

Copy for the "Sports of The Times" column is on Roach's desk. Tonight it's by Lipsyte, who writes about sports as another aspect of American life rather than simply fun and games. There's more to sports, he feels, than the crack of the bat against the ball, more than is seen from the press box. The

column he has just telephoned in from his home in the suburbs deals with the manipulation of athletes, specifically with
high school coaches who reach down into junior high schools
for talent and recruit twelve-year-olds for their schools. Lipsyte has pegged his column to a State Supreme Court case in
which a widowed mother brought suit to have her son rein-
stated on his high school basketball team after the Board of
Education asserted that the boy really didn't live where he
said he did and shouldn't be attending that school. Lipsyte attended the trial and has spent the last two weeks fleshing out
the story, talking to kids and coaches around the city. Today's
column is the first in a series.

• • •

At 2:22 P.M., the phone in the telephone recording room
rings. It's George Vecsey, calling from Fort Lauderdale. The
operator puts on his headset, throws a switch on a recording
machine connected to the telephone, and says, "Go ahead."
Vecsey dictates his story. When he has finished, he tells the operator, "That's all . . . O.K.?" There are no questions. Everything has come in clear. They hang up. The operator tran-
scribes the 500-word story, and within minutes it is on the
sports copydesk.

It was supposed to have been Vecsey's day off; spring training reporters work six days a week and take a day off when
no news seems imminent. But five Yankees, including Mickey
Mantle, are still absent from camp, so Vecsey decided he must
work.

"Mickey Mantle," he grumbled that morning as he gazed
from his window at the sparkling blue ocean at the motel's
doorstep. "Another day spent worrying about Mickey Mantle." Vecsey has been covering baseball for ten years, and he
and Mantle have never been friendly. But if Mantle shows up
at camp today, Vecsey will have to write a story about him.

First, a romp on the beach with his wife and two daughters
who are with him at spring training. At 10 A.M. he climbs into

his car and heads for the Fort Lauderdale Stadium. The players have just gotten into uniform. He notices that a uniform still hangs in Mantle's locker. That means he's still absent. But there are street clothes in Joe Pepitone's locker. Joe has reported.

Vecsey searches out Manager Ralph Houk. "Where's Mickey?" he asks.

"We expect him in uniform tomorrow," the manager replies; "at least that's what I'm told."

The Mantle situation is confused. He's been telling friends all winter that he will work out for a couple of weeks in spring training and then make up his mind whether to play another year. But to some people he has confided that he probably won't play any more.

Practice goes on until 1 o'clock. Vecsey watches it all, introduces himself to the new men, watches pitchers warm up in the bullpen, watches men practice new positions in the field, chats with the players around the batting cage. Joe Pepitone, shaggy-haired with long sideburns, and talking a mile a minute, shakes hands with all the reporters as he awaits his first swings of the year.

Vecsey plots his story in his mind as he drives back to his beach motel. Tomorrow he will write "Where is Mickey Mantle?" Today it will be Joe Pepitone, same old Joe, cutting up on his first day on the job.

That's the story he dictated into the 43d Street recording room. Then he called the sports desk, informed them of what he had filed and told them that Mantle was expected at camp the next day. He will delay his day off still another day to describe the first appearance in uniform of one of America's great heroes.

"Get all the good quotes," the deskman reminds him.

• • •

Today, Friday, sports deskmen are warming up for the Saturday push. They must put together the fifteen columns allotted for tonight's paper and get a head start on layouts and features for the Sunday "Sports" section, stealing a lead on tomorrow's deadline dash.

While the sports department, along with every other news classification, tries for as much space as possible in the weekday paper, it has no complaints about the eighty-or-so columns it averages in the Sunday paper. This is pure joy for the writers, who can let their stories run longer and have more turn-around room than when they write for the daily, but it's a mixed blessing for the editors.

Sunday "Sports" must be on the presses shortly before 6 P.M. on Saturday if it is to catch up with sections printed earlier and sent ahead, around the country, for Sunday morning distribution. Because so many events are still incomplete at that hour, "Sports" is the last of the Sunday sections to go to press, and its pages are opened up for late results and late events at least half a dozen times during the night.

No one in the sports department gets the day off on Saturday, whereas the other departments work the week end with short staffs. The main news section is ordinarily cleaned up early in the evening, barring an unexpected news break somewhere in the world, and a skeleton crew keeps the watch until the paper closes. But the sports staff fights the clock all through the night, working as fast at 2 A.M. preparing "live" copy for the final edition as it does for the first edition.

The timing on Saturday of the announcement of Mantle's retirement caught Vecsey and the sports staff in New York in an early-deadline vise. It was 8:30 in the morning when Bob Fishel, the Yankee publicity man, called Vecsey to announce "a big press conference concerning Mickey at three P.M."

"What's the news?" Vecsey asked him.

Fishel said he didn't know, that he was writing his press release both ways.

That sounded incredible to Vecsey. "Bob, I'm assuming that Mantle is quitting. We have an early Saturday deadline, and I've got to start writing something before the press conference begins."

Fishel thought that a good idea.

Vecsey called Jim Roach in New York and repeated the conversation. They agreed that Vecsey should prepare a feature story on Mantle's career and get it in as early as possible so it could be readied for the 5:30 first edition deadline. Then, if Mantle announced his retirement, Vecsey would quickly file what Roach calls "instant copy."

At 3:40 on Saturday afternoon, Vecsey broke from the crowded press conference at Yankee headquarters in Fort Lauderdale and made for the telephone. He dialed the 43d Street recording room and began to dictate:

"Mickey Mantle, one of baseball's greatest stars for the last 18 years, announced his retirement today at the spring training base of the New York Yankees."

His 1,200-word story led the "Sports" section of Sunday, March 2, accompanied by a full page of text and photos of Mantle's career.

· · · · 3 p.m.

Lewis Jordan has cut space requests to the bone and still has not gotten the total down to 200 columns. At 3 o'clock, Henry China appears at his desk. China is the publication manager, responsible for the positioning of all display advertising. The size of the paper must be firmly fixed at this hour.

"I've an unpleasant surprise for you," Jordan tells him. "It's 205."

"I've a pleasant surprise for *you*," China replies. "Our figure's 307."

This means that tomorrow's paper will carry 307 columns of advertising, 205 of news, for a total of 512 columns—a perfect sixty-four-page paper. It doesn't always work out this well. Sometimes the total number of columns doesn't add up to a paper that is mechanically possible to print. Then adjustments have to be made. Unless Jordan can pare his estimates, the excess is taken out of advertising. News requirements get prime consideration.

Jordan runs down the "open space" needs with China— three ad-free holes for the Sirhan trial, three for the Eshkol funeral. Ads will be shifted to make room for them. Space for the Eshkol funeral will be cleared in the front of the paper, on the pages devoted to foreign news; space for the Sirhan trial will be opened up on the national news pages that follow foreign news.

"And if Eisenhower dies before the second edition," Jordan tells China, "we'll need five clear pages, starting with a left-hand page." This will take care of the four-page prepared obituary plus a page of "live" news that will jump inside from the page 1 announcement of death.

China makes a note to check with Joseph Wagner, national advertising manager, and Warren Wolfe, retail advertising manager, for a list of ads to pull from the paper should it be necessary, between the first and second editions, to clear the pages for the obituary. The list will not include timely ads, such as the "today only" offerings of department stores. If anything has to give, it will be ads that can run just as well later.

. . .

The call goes out over the loud-speaker on the metropolitan desk: "Early summaries, please."

Every reporter is required to write a brief summary of the story he is working on for the guidance of the editors. Summaries come by cable from reporters abroad and by telephone from reporters around the country. Local reporters write them at their desks or, if they are in the field, telephone them into the recording room.

The metropolitan desk's call for early summaries is to fill in Arthur Gelb on exactly what is coming, to prepare him for the 4 o'clock conference in the managing editor's office when each desk head will run through the major stories expected from his bailiwick.

Gelb and his assistants, an hour earlier, had conferred with their counterparts on the nightside—Sheldon Binn and George Barrett, assistant metropolitan editors, who report in early afternoon and stay until midevening. Their job is to prepare the local news report for publication. Gelb and his aides brief them on what has been assigned, and to whom. Some stories assigned this morning have been scratched from the schedule, or altered if they shaped up differently than was anticipated. Others have been added.

Reporters returning from assignment line up to report to Binn, a genial, thoroughly professional man whose enthusiasm for his craft is so contagious that he is highly respected by the staff, a curious position for an editor. Each reporter gives him a quick rundown of how his story will shape up.

"What's your lead?" Binn asks, if he has not already read the reporter's summary. He either concurs with the writer or suggests alternatives, and they finally reach agreement. Binn then tells the reporter how much to write. This is generally good for an argument. The reporter almost always wants more space; the editor is always trying to hold it down. He sees the whole desk's picture; the reporter bleeds for his own story. Occasionally, though, it works the other way. Homer Bigart, the cynical, consummate pro, reported to Binn one day: "This story's so dull it *must* be important."

At 3:05 a United Press International bulletin reaches the metropolitan desk. It says: "Gas explosion in 7-story apartment house, Rockaway Beach."

Martin Arnold, a general assignment reporter, is summoned to the desk and informed that Ernest Sisto, a news photographer, will meet him in the lobby and they should proceed with all possible speed to the Rockaway address.

They make the one-hour run to the explosion scene in Queens in Sisto's car. They find a small cluster of housing development cops.

"What's it all about?" Arnold asks the cops.

"Nothing," they tell him. A concrete wall in the housing development's incinerator room buckled. No damage.

Arnold finds a phone and calls Binn. "No story," he reports. Binn scratches it from the schedule.

The reporter and photographer turn around and start the drive back to 43d Street.

A three-hour chase after a nonexistent story is part of the day's work. Reporters often spend their time going after what turns out to be a nonstory. Editors cannot take the chance of not having a man at a possible disaster scene.

But sometimes a man finds himself much busier than he thought he'd be. Seth S. King, a City Hall reporter, had expected a quiet day. Friday usually is. Mayor Lindsay was not in his office, and most city departments had shut early for the week end. No press conferences were scheduled; there were no City Council or Board of Estimate meetings.

The three-man Times bureau at City Hall generally spends Friday checking through the building to see if there are any statements, announcements, committee meetings or the like that they should pursue. Today there is nothing. By midafternoon the outlook for news is bleak. Martin Tolchin, chief of the City Hall bureau, is with the Mayor on an inspection tour of subway construction and maintenance. Tolchin will not return to Room 9, the City Hall press room. He will write his story from the 43d Street newsroom.

At 3:15, without warning, Robert Laird, Mayor Lindsay's assistant press secretary, walks into Room 9 and tells the reporters the Mayor has an important announcement. Laird passes around a statement saying that the city has reached an agreement with the State, County and Municipal Employes Union on an agency shop.

Seth King pores over the Mayor's statement. He realizes the story has implications. It is the first time the city has ever agreed to require all civil servants who are not members of the union to pay a "service fee" equivalent to union dues. But the story also has a lot of what Charles Bennett, the third member of the City Hall bureau and its fiscal expert, calls "booby traps." There is no information on exactly how many people will be affected by the agreement, how many other unions may come in on it, what it may mean in bargaining on future city contracts.

King calls Binn on the metropolitan desk to outline the story, and it is added to the schedule. Then he gets on the phone to track down the missing information. But it is Friday afternoon; most of the people who know the answers have left for the week end. He finally reaches union headquarters and gets enough information to flesh out the bare bones of the Mayor's announcement. He rides the subway uptown to 43d Street to write the story there.

· · ·

At 3:30 Binn takes a call from Barnard Collier in Plainfield, New Jersey. Collier, a general assignment reporter, had been sent out from the newsroom at noon, hard on receipt of an Associated Press bulletin about a confrontation between blacks and whites at an impromptu meeting in a high school auditorium. He had driven across the Hudson River in a Times car, one of a fleet garaged next door to the 43d Street plant for just such emergencies. Now he tells Binn:

"Six kids have been arrested. They expect several hundred people to show up with grievances later. There might be more trouble tonight."

Binn tells him to stick with the story for another hour or so, then return to the office to write it. Robert Smith, a rewrite man due in at 6 o'clock, will be dispatched instead to Plainfield to cover whatever trouble occurs later and phone inserts to the story.

· · ·

Abe Rosenthal has stayed close to the action all day. He gives the impression of tremendous energy expertly controlled as he moves between his own desk at the hub of newsroom activity and the desks of the foreign, national and metropolitan editors.

He stops by the national desk. "Anything big?" he asks.

"Just Ike," Gene Roberts tells him.

Rosenthal suggests some changes in the short version of the Ike obit, the one that will be slipped into the paper as a holdover until tomorrow should he die after the midnight edition has gone to press.

"We ought to get in the bit about his being a great figure, grandfather of the country and all that," Rosenthal suggests. Roberts calls Bob Phelps, the Washington bureau news editor, and tells him to make sure this bit is included in the piece that Felix Belair is updating.

Belair is on the phone to his private medical sources and is scribbling notes on the serious setback to the former President's convalescence. Phelps stops by his desk and passes on the suggestion from Rosenthal. Belair makes the requested inserts and begins to write a pneumonia story, larding it with a brief recap of the General's earlier heart attacks.

. . .

In an adjoining nook in the bureau's plush newsroom, Ben Welles, after a multi-Scotch lunch, finds on his desk a message from Gerald Gold on the foreign desk: "Please check out State Department reaction to Soviet note to the East Germans."

From its 43d Street command post the foreign desk is piecing together the various angles of the Soviet note story. It is in communication with its correspondents in all the world's capitals where the note has implications.

At 3:07, Topping gets a message from Lewis in London: BINDER WANTS YOU TO CALL HIM RIGHT AWAY AT BERLIN BUREAU. Topping asks The Times's switchboard to place an urgent call to Berlin. The connection is immediate. Binder wants to talk about the new lead on his story slugged "Facedown." He does not feel that the Soviet note signals a major crisis in East-West relations. He believes the Communist stance is relatively restrained. Topping is inclined to agree and instructs him to write it as he sees it. But should an emergency occur, Topping tells him that correspondents in Central Europe have been alerted to get to Germany as quickly as possible to assist in coverage.

While Topping is on the phone to Berlin, Gold gets off a

In the wire room, adjacent to the newsroom, teleprinters punch out copy from all over the country and all over the world. Clerks strip it from the machines and distribute it to the news desks that will handle it. *(Photo by Lee Romero)*

Stories are prepared for publication at horseshoe-shaped copydesks. Copyreaders check and verify facts, clarify sentences and write headlines. The chief of the foreign desk, the slot man, is facing the camera. *(Photo by Larry Frank)*

In the composing room, edited copy is converted into type. Some copy is set on standard line-casting machines: The operator taps out the characters on a typewriterlike keyboard, and the machine casts them into lines of molten metal, which harden quickly into cold type.

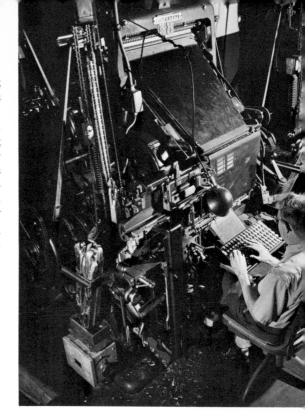

Other copy is set on teletypesetters. These machines are also equipped with keyboards, but instead of typing letters they punch holes in a tape. The coded tape is then fed into line-casting machines and emerges as metal lines. *(Photo by Larry Frank)*

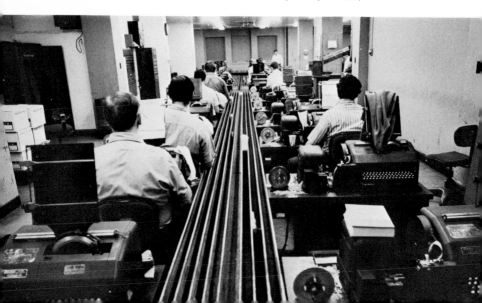

The lines of type, assembled in metal trays, or galleys, are carried to make-up tables, where printers, working from page dummies, place them in their allocated spaces in the page forms. When everything is in place—news, ads, headlines, illustrations—the pages are locked up and carried to mat machines, where cardboard matrices are molded. The mats are dropped down a chute to the stereotype shop in the subbasement pressroom.

The mats go into plate-casting machines, which reproduce the flat type and pictures on curved metal plates. The plates, with page numbers inked boldly on their surface, crawl along the floor on mechanical conveyer belts to the waiting presses. There they are locked into place on the press cylinders.

Giant newsprint rolls stacked in the reel room (foreground) are threaded into position (rear) and fed through the presses, one floor above. Each roll of paper is five miles long. Automatic "flying pasters" splice spent rolls to fresh, so that once a press starts to roll, the sheets move through it in a continuous flow.

Streams of printed and folded papers pour from the presses and climb in continuous line through spring-wire escalators to the mail room, one floor above, at street level.

There they are automatically stacked, tied into bundles and whisked
by conveyer into waiting delivery trucks backed up at loading platforms. *(Photo by Larry Morris)*

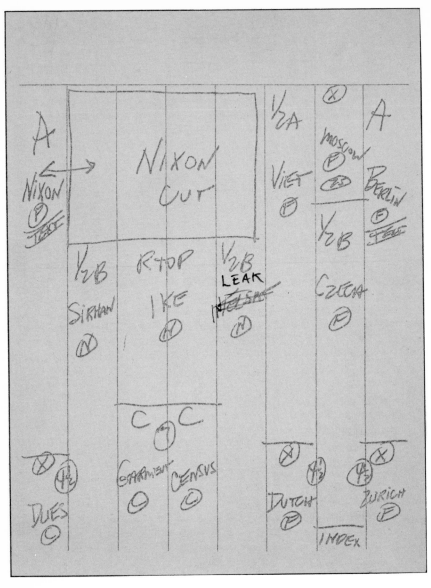

Front-page dummy for The Times of March 1, 1969. Similar diagrams are made for every page to guide make-up editors and printers as they fit the pieces into the page forms.

cable to Frankel in Paris: ASSUME SEMPLE WILL NOTE
AND TAKE ACCOUNT OF LATEST BERLIN DEVEL-
OPMENTS INCLUDING SOVIET NOTE WHICH WOULD
MEAN PARTIAL BLOCKADE. DOES UNISTATES
PLAN DIPLOMATIC INTERVENTION WITH RUS-
SIANS?

At 3:54 Kamm cables from Moscow: FULL TEXT OF
SOVIET NOTE TO EAST GERMANS AVAILABLE
HERE. IF TEXT UNAVAILABLE IN NEW YORK WE
CAN GIVE IT TO YOU. PLEASE ADVISE SOONEST.

Gold cables back: FORGET TEXT. WE HAVE IT. WANT
FROM YOU INTERPRETIVE MATERIAL ON WHAT IT
ALL PRESUMABLY MEANS.

Kamm has been trying to find out what it all means since
he received Gold's first message an hour earlier.

He has spoken to the American chargé d'affaires, the man
who hinted at his briefing this afternoon that a Communist-
sparked crisis might be developing. The chargé doesn't know
yet what to make of the note, but it must be taken seriously,
he says.

Kamm has tried to reach his contacts in the French, West
German and British Embassies. It's getting on toward midnight in Moscow, the peak of the evening for the diplomatic
corps, which dines late and leisurely, and he hasn't been able
to flush out his men at their homes or Embassies.

He finally makes contact with a British diplomat who "as-
sumes" that the British Embassy has received a copy of the
note because the Embassy guard told him on the phone that
an envelope had been delivered. But he cannot be sure it is
the same note until the envelope is opened.

"When will it be opened?" Kamm asks.

"Tomorrow morning," the diplomat replies.

"O.K.," Kamm tells him, "I'll write that the British diplomats think they have the same note, but they won't check it
until tomorrow morning."

The diplomat gets the message. He will stop at the Embassy

on his way home from the party, open the envelope and call back.

Kamm finally reaches his French friend at a dinner at the French Ambassador's residence. Yes, the French have received the note. A high Soviet official and the West German Ambassador are at the same dinner, and the subject is being discussed. Nothing very startling in the conversation, the Frenchman tells Kamm, and promises to get in touch with him if anything important develops.

Kamm hasn't much to write, but he goes with what he has: The Soviet note caused Western diplomats in Moscow to revise a professed optimism that there would be no full-fledged Berlin crisis. He places a call to the London bureau and dictates his 400-word story into a recorder for transmission to New York.

He hangs around the bureau for a while to see whether Tass will put any further details of the note on its wire. It doesn't. The Tass report is still skimpy and provides nothing new to add to his story. He turns out the lights, locks the office and steps out into the inky, frigid night. The office gets stuffy after a long stretch with the windows sealed against the icy drafts, and a brief walk in the fresh air will be invigorating. Makes for better sleeping.

. . .

Jim Feron has put in a long day, too, in Jerusalem. Shortly after 8 P.M. (when it was 1 P.M. in New York) he finished writing his story on the Eshkol funeral. He carried it to the censor and then to the post office, from which it was sent by telex through the London bureau to New York. That, he thought, would wind up his workday. Besides, it is Shabbat, the Jewish sabbath, and almost everything in Israel is shut tight from sundown Friday until sundown Saturday.

Today is the Ferons' wedding anniversary, and they have been invited to spend the evening with friends. Before leaving home, Jim turned on Kol Israel, the government radio station, to catch the 8:30 P.M. newscast, the second English-language broadcast of the day.

The first news item shattered his plans for an anniversary celebration. The announcer said: "Robert Finch, the American Secretary of Health, Education and Welfare, said today that President Nixon was planning to visit Israel."

Shattered, too, was Feron's desire not to disturb Israeli officials on the sabbath. He called the director of Jerusalem's Public Information Office at his home, the man who, earlier in the day, had barred him from entering Acting Premier Allon's office with the American delegation to the Eshkol funeral. The director had promised to call him if anything of substance came out of that meeting. He had not called.

Feron asked him, somewhat testily: "What about this Nixon visit?"

The PIO director was flabbergasted. "What Nixon visit?" he wanted to know.

Feron told him what Kol Israel had reported. The director promised to check it out and call right back. He did, to say that the Foreign Ministry was in a flap, that it knew nothing of any Nixon visit and that perhaps Kol Israel had gone a bit too hard on what Finch might have told one of their reporters were Nixon's hopes to visit Israel.

Feron called the spokesman for the American Embassy in Tel Aviv. Embassy officials, he learned, knew of no plans for a Nixon visit. The impression had apparently grown from what was intended to be a gracious remark by Mr. Finch.

Another phone call from the PIO director informed Feron that Kol Israel has been instructed to tone down its next broadcast.

"Have the agencies picked it up?" Feron asked. "Yes," the director told him, "the agencies have already sent out bulletins on the original announcement."

Feron knew he had to act fast. Agency bulletins reaching the foreign desk in New York announcing that Nixon planned

to visit Israel would, he knew, set off a barrage of cabled queries from Topping or Gold. He decided to call New York and
head them off.

. . .

It is a few minutes before 4 o'clock in New York when Gerald
Gold answers his phone and is told by the operator to hold for
a call from Jerusalem. Feron comes on and explains the origin
of the announcement as he has been able to piece it together
from officials. Gold tells him that he will ask Frankel, in Paris
with Nixon, to check it out; that, meanwhile, Feron should
file a couple of paragraphs on the stir caused in Israel by the
announcement. Feron hangs up and taps out on his typewriter: "Robert H. Finch . . . created a brief stir here tonight
by suggesting that President Nixon intended to visit Israel.
American and Israeli officials said later that they knew of no
plan for any such trip and suggested the impression had
grown from what was intended to be merely a gracious
remark. . . ."

Gold cables Frankel in Paris: FERON TELLS US AND
IS FILING SHORT THAT FINCH IN ISRAEL TODAY
CREATED FLAP BY SAYING NIXON INTENDS TO
VISIT ISRAEL EARLY IN HIS ADMINISTRATION. U.S.
PEOPLE THERE ARE POOPOOING BUT SO FAR AS WE
KNOW FINCH'S REMARKS HAVEN'T BEEN DENIED.
KNOW YOU ANYTHING?

The query reaches Frankel in the Paris bureau as he and
Henry Tanner are about to go out for a late dinner. He makes
a few phone calls, then replies to Gold: SOURCES HERE
KNOW OF NO PLAN FOR ISRAEL VISIT BUT THEY
SEE NOTHING TO DENY EITHER, ESPECIALLY
SINCE THEY UNINFORMED ON PRECISE FLAP.

. . .

Tanner, too, gets off a message to the foreign desk. An hour
or so earlier he had sent to New York the texts of the official
statements made by Nixon and de Gaulle at Orly Airport, and

Gold had shot back a query: ASSUME NIXON SPOKE IN ENGLISH AND DE GAULLE IN FRENCH AND THAT DE GAULLE'S IS OFFICIAL TRANSLATION.

YOU ARE RIGHT ON LANGUAGES, Tanner now replies, EXCEPT THAT DE GAULLE TRANSLATION IS UNOFFICIAL. NO OFFICIAL ONE AVAILABLE AS YET.

It's almost 10 o'clock in Paris. Frankel has written his piece for Sunday's "Week in Review" section, summarizing the accomplishments of the trip. He will have to wait until he returns from dinner to check out the foreign desk's query on whether the United States plans diplomatic intervention with Russia over the Soviet note that threatens at least a partial blockade of Berlin. Robert McCloskey, the State Department spokesman who can give him the answer, is attending the de Gaulle-Nixon dinner and can't be reached until the dinner breaks up.

Tom Wicker, having written and filed his column for Sunday's editorial page, has succumbed to the stomach distress that has plagued him along the tour and gone to his hotel, the Crillon, to bed. John Hess is typing out his fifth sidebar on Nixon's day in Paris. He has written a description of the Quai D'Orsay, where Nixon is staying. He has filed shorts on the demonstrations and violence that greeted the President, on a French opinion poll friendly to Nixon, on Nixon's handshaking efforts, and on the menu at the de Gaulle-Nixon dinner. The foreign desk will decide whether to include these short pieces in Bob Semple's lead story or run them separately.

Semple is batting out his story in the press room of the Hotel Georges Cinq, headquarters for reporters covering the Nixon trip. As he writes, a messenger picks up the pages, a couple at a time, and carries them across town by cycle to the Paris bureau for relay to New York. His lead is on the foreign desk in New York as he continues to pound away at his typewriter in Paris.

The Race to Deadline

········ 4 p.m.

The news this Friday afternoon is no better or no worse than usual. The new President is on a good-will tour of Europe; a former President lies dying; an East-West crisis threatens; an ugly war drags on; two trials of world-wide interest grind slowly to a climax.

At 4 o'clock the editors of the major news desks take their seats again, as they had this morning, around the long oak table in the managing editor's office. This time they are joined by the bullpen editors who, with Rosenthal, will lay out page 1 less than two hours from now. The meeting is called to bring everyone up to date quickly on what has happened this day in the world, the nation and the city. Listening in are the publisher, the circulation director and the promotion director. The publisher is there simply because he wants to be kept informed of what is going on. The circulation director sits in to learn if there is a story of special interest to a particular community. If there is, he will pad (increase) deliveries of the paper in that area. The promotion director will prepare newsstand posters or radio spots if a specific story warrants a plug for readers' attention.

Abe Rosenthal, who presides at the meeting, knows pretty much what to expect even before his editors begin their rundowns of stories for tomorrow's paper. All day he has kept an eye on the news ticker at his desk and has been in continual contact with the editors of the various news subdivisions. First, the day's foreign news developments. He signals to Seymour Topping.

Topping reads from the sheaf of summaries in front of him:

"A note has been sent by the Soviet Union to the East Germans charging that strategic war materials are being produced in West Berlin and authorizing the East Germans to take whatever steps it deems necessary to halt what it terms illegal military activities in Western Germany."

"Is this a new charge?" Rosenthal asks.

"They may have said something like it in the past," Topping replies, "but in this context they are obviously trying to say it's their right to stop materials and look at them. It could represent a partial blockade or serious harassment on goods going overland. The framework of the threat is obviously the election which is scheduled for Wednesday."

Rosenthal interjects: "We've got to have an assessment of this from Washington on how seriously it's taken."

Topping: "I've asked for it, and also from Moscow and from the traveling White House in Paris. I have talked to Binder on the phone, and he expressed an opinion similar to my own; he doesn't believe there's going to be a great crunch on this. But you can't tell about these things. From my own experience when I was in Berlin, the danger is that there will be a miscalculation by either side which could result in some kind of serious flare-up."

Ted Bernstein, the assistant managing editor who is the liaison between the bullpen editors and Reston, Daniel and Rosenthal, the top newsroom brass, asks: "Are the Russians charging a violation of the Potsdam Treaty?"

Topping: "I don't know specifically, though there's a provision in the treaty that the Germans are not supposed to do this. But it's been violated by both East and West Germany in the production of their own war goods. We'll go into that."

Topping continues his rundown of foreign stories: Drew Middleton in Brussels on the circumstances under which the Allies would use nuclear weapons . . . Tad Szulc in Bucharest on the upcoming Rumanian elections . . . Jonathan Randal in Prague on the Czechs' rejection of the Brezhnev doctrine of limited sovereignty . . . Nixon's arrival in Paris and the apparent motivation of the two sides, and a clean-up story from Bob Doty in Rome on the result of the talks there . . . two stories relating to the Roman Catholic Church, one from Vienna, the other from The Hague . . . the fighting in Vietnam . . . an exclusive from Paul Hofmann in Paris that Nixon will receive Ky Sunday morning . . . and on the second front a color story from John Hess on the move to the suburbs of Les Halles, the food basket of Paris.

That winds up the foreign news report. Rosenthal signals to Gene Roberts, national news editor.

Roberts: "President Eisenhower, as we know, caught pneumonia during the night and had difficulty breathing and this morning was described as generally weaker. Another bulletin is expected in an hour and a half. What we plan to do as part of the Ike story tonight, if he does not die, is to have a bit of background on how this is part of a long battle for survival. If he does die, then we'll have a separate story recounting all his medical difficulties.

"Bill Blair in Washington is doing a story saying that the Secretary of the Interior has urged stronger legislation than presently proposed to protect offshore waters from any pollution by oil wells. When he made these recommendations before the Senate Public Works subcommittee this morning, he was warmly commended that he had taken action.

"Down in New Orleans, the Clay Shaw trial is moving toward the jury.

"In the *Pueblo* hearing, crewmen today have given testimony strongly commending Commander Bucher and once again bringing up the issue that the big crime was not Bucher's leadership but the fact that the Navy didn't come to his rescue."

Rosenthal: "Any end in sight?"

Roberts: "Not right now."

At this point, Executive Editor James Reston enters the meeting. He rarely attends these 4 o'clock rundown sessions, but today he has a point he wants to get across.

"Have you talked about foreign affairs yet?" he asks.

He learns that the foreign report has been completed.

"We ought to put out a dragnet for the official version of the de Gaulle-Nixon talks that the French will send to the Embassy," he says. "The most important potential leak we can get out of the trip would be what they said to each other. Let's try to get the diplomatic report."

Reston leaves the room.

The rundown of stories continues. It's Metropolitan Editor Arthur Gelb's turn. He reads from the summaries before him.

"Mayor Lindsay has criticized the Transit Authority for delays in subway construction and maintenance. He says that trying to get a response out of the Transit Authority is like trying to get an echo out of the Grand Canyon.

"We've got reporters out at five high schools. There's been interracial fighting at all these schools. We're trying to find out what's going on. Part of the attacks have been blacks on whites and whites on blacks. But I don't know yet what form the story will take. It might be one big wrap-up, or it might be separate stories."

Rosenthal: "I think you'd better make it one big wrap-up."

Gelb: "Also, out in Plainfield, New Jersey, six pupils were arrested today in a shouting, fist-swinging melee that erupted in the auditorium of Plainfield High School. The school was closed at 9:30 this morning. They had been airing Negro demands when the fist fighting broke out.

"The airlines are operating, absorbing the overflow from the struck American Airlines without major difficulty, and

there's very little going on in the way of negotiations. . . .
Two former detectives who were on the Narcotics Squad were
sentenced in Federal Court today to eight years in prison on
charges of selling narcotics. The judge said: 'Words can't be
found for such a hideous crime.'. . . . Another unusual story:
Local 259 of the United Auto Workers announced full and
fighting support for the Ocean Hill-Brownsville idea of community control of the schools. The president of the union said
they'd carry their fight to Albany."

That's the local news picture as of this hour. John G. Morris, the picture editor, reports that he has agency pictures in
hand of President Nixon in Rome and "specials" coming in by
wire on the burial of Premier Eshkol in Israel.

"That's it," Rosenthal says. The meeting is over. It is 4:15.
The editors shove back their chairs, gather up their notes and
hurry to their desks. The signal now is "go." The push to
deadline is on.

• • •

The newsroom is filling up. The seats around the horseshoe-
shaped copydesks are almost all occupied. Copyreaders, heads
bowed, ballpoint pens skimming, are processing early stories
and sending them by pneumatic tube to the composing room,
one floor above, to be set in type.

The flow of copy to the composing room must be smooth,
orderly and strictly regulated if an edition is to go to press on
time. Today, the first live copy reached the composing room
shortly after 2 o'clock, from the foreign desk, which is invariably first because time works in its favor. Early copy from all
desks—stories that can be written before the last moment—
must be set in type in late afternoon, clearing composing-
room decks for the final big rush of spot news. If copy were
permitted to pile up in the hour or two before closing, it
would be mechanically impossible to meet the split-second
timing of an edition deadline.

By 4:15 the foreign copydesk has cleared about one-half of

its stories. The national copydesk, with time working against it, has less than one-third of its eighteen-column quota in hand. Nothing is in yet from California, where, at 1 P.M., there is still half a day to go in the *Pueblo* hearing and the Sirhan trial. Chick Butsikares, the assistant national news editor who pulls together the national news report and steers it through the copydesk, knows that Bernard Weinraub in Coronado and Douglas Robinson in San Francisco will just barely make the first edition. He knows, too, that it will be another hour at least before Martin Waldron begins to file his account of the day's proceedings at the Shaw trial in New Orleans. There is nothing in yet from the Washington bureau. That copy will start hurtling in about 6 o'clock over the high-speed transmitter that links the bureau with the 43d Street wire room.

. . .

Among the early stories on the national desk is one by John Noble Wilford, aerospace reporter, from Cape Kennedy, Florida. It is not the piece Wilford had expected to file, but it's not his fault.

A great news story had been expected from Cape Kennedy today. All the rockets and the spacecraft were ready for the Apollo 9 mission, the first test of the lunar module and the last practice flight in earth's orbit before men set out for the landing on the moon. But yesterday the three astronauts came down with colds, and NASA announced a three-day delay in the launch.

Wilford has covered so many launchings that Room 109 at the Ramada Inn, where he always stays, has become a sort of mini-Times bureau for space shots. He goes to Cape Kennedy a week before a scheduled blast-off to cover the long countdown. After he writes the story of the lift-off, he catches a plane to Houston, the focal point of the mission once it is off the ground. There he joins other Times science writers assigned to various technical angles of the flight.

The Ramada always gives Wilford Room 109 because it is equipped with an Associated Press printer and with a special telephone that enables him to place calls direct without tangling with the inn's overworked switchboard. The Times also maintains an old house trailer set up at the press site on the Cape. This provides a haven from the sun, air conditioning for the countdowns, a special telephone connected to the 43d Street recording room, and two television sets, one for regular commercial TV, the other closed-circuit coverage of the astronauts as they leave their quarters, go to the pad and enter the spacecraft.

But the trailer is for launch day, and there will be no launch today. So Wilford stays in Cocoa Beach, the strip of motels, restaurants and night spots that is the center of life at Apollo shots.

Shortly after noon he had called the national desk in New York to give Irv Horowitz a brief report on the health of the Apollo crew. He had tried to check out a rumor that the astronauts were not sick with colds; they were simply exhausted, and some NASA officials were beginning to feel that preflight training was too rigorous. He had been assured that the men did have colds, but he also got hints that there might be some truth to the debate about their training regimen. He could not say it in today's story, he told Horowitz, but his story would reflect it.

At 2:30, he telephoned a summary into the 43d Street recording room for delivery to the national news desk. Then, after a swim in the Ramada pool, he began to write. His 650 words, dictated and transcribed, are now on the national copydesk.

· · ·

The sea of formica-topped reporters' desks is filling. Beat men have come in to write the stories that have emanated from the downtown public offices to which they are assigned—City Hall, the municipal departments, the courts. General assignment reporters and the specialists—men who cover politics, labor, crime, race, religion—are at their desks, making calls, taking calls, organizing notes, skimming through wire-service copy related to their stories that has piled up during the day. The muted ring of telephones, the clackity-clack of typewriters are the overt signs that deadline pressure is building.

The early rewrite men—Lawrence Van Gelder and Murray Illson—have taken their places in the front row of desks directly north of the metropolitan desk. Before the night is out, there will be six men in this front-line phalanx.

Rewrite men are the newspaper's sentinels against disaster. They come to work as the day fades and stay until the last "good night" is given. They are the metropolitan desk's backstop against poorly written or inadequately covered stories; they recoup on stories that should have been assigned but weren't. They knock out stories on late-breaking news from notes telephoned in by men in the field. They rarely leave their desks. Their principal tools are the telephone, a handful of clippings, a file of valuable contacts, from which they fashion running stories, reactions, profiles, obituaries, sidebars, inserts and background. There is always a short ration of time for rewrite men, yet their stories are indistinguishable from those of men on the scene.

Almost before Van Gelder has shed his topcoat, jacket and vest, stopped at his mailbox and settled down at his desk, he is approached by Mike Stern, an assistant metropolitan editor. Stern informs him that there has been a snafu, that no one has covered, or is prepared to write about, the Mayor's announcement of the establishment of an experimental program called the Pre-Arraignment Processing Facility, situated in the Bronx. Stern drops some wire-service copy about the Mayor's announcement on Van Gelder's desk. Van Gelder glances at it. He is not prepared to write about the Pre-Arraignment Processing Facility; he's never even heard of it. Martin Tolchin, the chief City Hall reporter, comes by on his way to report to

Sheldon Binn. Van Gelder stops him and asks who in the Mayor's office can fill him in. Tolchin tells him whom to call.

Reporters approach Binn in steady stream to go over their stories and get their space allotments.

"I was in Canarsie with Lindsay on the Transit story," Tolchin tells him. "The Mayor's passing the buck. People on the street asked him why he was there, and he said to show his concern for the new railroad station that should have been built two years ago. But the Transit Authority says that's not true, that the Mayor took the trip after Transit complained it was not getting enough money. The Mayor says his worst problems are with two of the biggest departments in the city —Education and Transit—over which he has no control."

Binn: "Maybe the lead should be the Mayor's complaint that he has no control over two of the biggest departments in the city."

Tolchin: "He only mentioned schools tangentially. I'll make the point in the third or fourth paragraph."

The guts of the story, they agree, is that the Mayor took this opportunity to tee off on the Transit Authority.

"Give me a dollar," Binn says—one way of asking for a column. "And slug it 'Lindsay.' "

Richard Reeves, the metropolitan staff's chief political reporter, is next in line. "I'm on the schedule," he tells Binn, "but it's not going to work out." Reeves has been trying to flesh out a story about the half-dozen or so Democratic candidates for Mayor angling for the endorsement of Senator Ted Kennedy. "I can't get to Kennedy until Monday," he reports. Binn scratches the story from the schedule. It will be rescheduled next week.

Damon Stetson, the staff's chief labor reporter, checks in. "Not a hell of a lot happening on the American Airlines strike. The other airlines are taking up the slack. No negotiations."

"Half a column," Binn orders.

Peter Millones has returned from Columbia with answers to the questions Gelb asked this morning about the University's plans for a new gym. He tells Binn: "Several sites are under consideration, but there will be no commitment without approval of community leaders. Meanwhile, they're going to replace the trees they tore down in Morningside Park before protesters forced them to abandon their original plan. They might even landscape the park if the community thinks it's a good idea."

Binn tells him to write three-quarters of a column.

C. Gerald Fraser, back from Harlem, where he covered a legislative committee hearing on crime, reports: "Neighborhood kids say the cops not only know that drugs are being sold but peddle drugs themselves to make a little extra money."

"Let's put the lead on the kids," Binn says, "on what they say about the cops. Then tie in the Federal Court conviction today of two former cops on narcotics charges. Slug it 'Narco,' and let's have a column."

. . .

In the composing room, proof boys lift chases—black metal page forms—from their storage racks and place them on stones—steel make-up tables. Beneath each empty, yawning chase a printer chalks a number—1 to 64—the number of pages in tomorrow's paper.

A parade of turtles—metal-wheeled tables—piled high with advertisements moves slowly toward the stones. The various parts of each ad—the metal engraving and the metal type—have been assembled and put together on advertising make-up banks, and just before 5 o'clock they are wheeled out to the page forms they are scheduled to fill.

Ray Nelan and John Fiala, who made up the advertising page dummies, or scratches, earlier in the afternoon, are in the composing room now, directing the proof boys with their heavy metal loads to the designated pages. At the stones, printers, working from the dummies, begin to place the ads in their indicated positions. They want to get the ads in the forms before the rush of news type begins.

The full-page ad directed to page 64, the back page of tomorrow's paper, will be a rerun of an ad for *Avant Garde,* the far-out magazine published by the controversial Ralph Ginzburg. Mr. Ginzburg had reserved the page for an ad in which he planned to use a picture of Supreme Court Justice William O. Douglas and a plug for an article the Justice had written for *Avant Garde,* called "An Appeal to Folk Singing: A Landmark Opinion." This morning Mr. Ginzburg had called Vincent Redding, manager of The Times's Advertising Acceptability department, to say that the ad was set to go, that Justice Douglas had given permission to use his picture. All appeared in order, but Mr. Redding, a cautious man, decided to call the Justice's office in Washington as a double check. And just as well. The Justice's secretary informed him there had been a mistake. Permission had been granted at first, but had subsequently been withdrawn. Mr. Redding immediately informed Mr. Ginzburg of the changed signals from Washington. Mr. Ginzburg had made an honest mistake. There had been a slip-up, and he had not been informed that the Justice had changed his mind. By now time was running out, and there was nothing for *Avant Garde* to do with its reserved space but substitute a subscription-seeking ad it had run four months earlier. That ad is now placed in the page 64 chase.

Another late-in-the-day substitution, because of Mr. Redding's watchfulness, is a page 2 ad for Richter's, a Fifth Avenue jewelry store. Mr. Redding had winced this morning when he read the original Richter's copy. It said: "Buy her ring at Richter's . . . and if you want, get the gift box across the street." The "across the street" jab was obviously aimed at Tiffany. Mr. Redding sternly informed Richter's that the copy violated The Times's rule that retail advertisers must confine their remarks to their own operations and avoid reference to other stores. Richter's argued that Tiffany and Bonwit Teller were both across the street, and this, they believed, diluted direct or objectionable references to another store. But Mr. Redding held firm. He would not permit the ad to run, he told Richter's, without Tiffany's permission. A call to Tiffany left no doubt that this was not forthcoming. So Richter's reluctantly changed its copy to read: "At Richter's, you pay for what's in the box, not the name on it."

Every display ad in The Times comes under the scrutiny of Mr. Redding and his associates. They reword, revise or toss out altogether advertisements they consider misleading, inaccurate, or unfairly competitive or offensive to good taste. If they run across anything questionable—exaggerated phraseology, unwarranted claims, improper illustrations—they call the advertiser and discuss the offending copy. Most of the time a mutually satisfactory revision is worked out, as it was today, after some sparring, with Richter's.

The job calls for tact and judgment. Just this afternoon Mr. Redding politely turned down a record company executive who called to ask if The Times would accept a small ad in which the executive wanted to accuse a restaurant of discourtesy. Mr. Redding didn't even wait to hear the details before he said no. Then he softened the rebuff by pointing out that not only was libel involved, but if The Times accepted ads criticizing individuals or institutions for discourtesy, there would be no end to requests for space. The executive hadn't thought about that. He hung up, satisfied with Mr. Redding's rejection.

· · · · · · · 5 p.m.

On the foreign, national and metropolitan desks, the editors confer among themselves to determine which stories they will recommend for page 1.

The foreign desk has most of its principal stories in hand. Binder's revised copy is in from Berlin. It begins: "The Soviet Union and its ally, East Germany, threatened tonight to impose restrictions on traffic on the lifeline access routes between West Berlin and West Germany."

A good part of Bob Semple's story is in from Paris. It starts off: "Calling for an end to 'old slogans' and 'old quarrels,' President Nixon arrived in Paris today for the last and most difficult phase of his eight-day effort to repair the worn fabric of the North Atlantic Treaty Alliance." Not much hard news there, Topping and Gold agree. They decide that the Berlin crisis should be their top-story recommendation, not Nixon in Paris as they had thought earlier in the day.

Semple would have agreed with this decision. Protected by the six-hour time difference, he has dawdled and procrastinated. It's a difficult story to write because no real news has come out of the day's activities. It's after 11 o'clock when he gets up from his typewriter. The copy should all be in New York by now, he realizes with a twinge of guilt. The press room in the Hotel Georges Cinq is empty save for Charles

Bailey of *The Minneapolis Tribune,* who is busily pounding away. Has he learned something hot, Semple wonders?

"Good story?" he asks Bailey with feigned unconcern.

"Impossible," Bailey grumbles. "It's always impossible when you don't have anything to sink your teeth into." He throws Semple his lead. It begins: "Calling for an end to 'old slogans' and 'old quarrels,' President Nixon arrived . . ."

Semple feels better.

• • •

At the metropolitan desk, Gelb and Binn confer with the five reporters who have returned from covering interracial fighting in the city's schools. It's apparent that the biggest scene was at Andrew Jackson High in Queens—forty cops called in to keep the peace.

"You write the wrap-up," Gelb tells Leonard Buder, who has been at Andrew Jackson.

"And hold it to a column and a half," Binn adds.

The other reporters go to their desks to type up their notes. They will turn them over to Buder to incorporate in his wrap-up. Gelb will make a pitch for page 1 display, but his best bet tonight is Peter Kihss's survey on how blacks are faring in the cities. Another possibility: Seth King's piece from City Hall about the first agency shop for municipal employes.

• • •

Larry Hauck, the assistant news editor who at this hour must select the "Quotation of the Day," has glanced through all the incoming copy as it piled up in the bullpen baskets and decided that his idea earlier this afternoon was a good one. He found a nifty quote in the story from Albany on the Department of Education's decision to permit girls to participate with boys in noncontact sports. It says: "In a limited number of experiences that have come to our attention wherein girls competed on boys' teams, the only negative feature reported is that it is not yet socially acceptable for a girl to defeat a boy in athletic competition." It fits all his specifications: It's attributable, brief, significant and provides contrast to the rather ponderous tone of tonight's news. The story will be handled by the metropolitan desk, as is all New York State copy, so Hauck informs the slot man on the metropolitan copydesk of his selection. He wants to make sure the sentence will not be deleted or altered in the editing process.

· · ·

The national desk, with time working against it, has a less clear picture at 5 o'clock of how its stories will shape up. Bernard Weinraub's first-edition story from Coronado, California, on the *Pueblo* hearing is coming in by Western Union. Nothing startling there. Another morning of testimony by crew members. Unless the afternoon session yields something more newsworthy, the *Pueblo* story is not a candidate for page 1.

From New Orleans, Martin Waldron has filed 700 words summing up the State's closing arguments in the Clay Shaw conspiracy trial. Waldron has called the national desk to say that the court will reconvene for an evening session to hear the summation by the defense, and the judge has said he will give the case to the jury tonight, if possible. Not front page for early editions; but if a verdict is reached before last-edition closing, it will be moved outside.

The morning session of the Sirhan trial in Los Angeles had been, according to Douglas Robinson in a telephone call to the national desk, "dull, dull, dull," taken up with testimony by a boyhood friend of Sirhan's about life in Jerusalem for the Arabs in 1948.

After lunch Robinson repairs to the press room in the Hall of Justice building, four floors below the courtroom, to write a story for the first edition. There's no real news. He mulls over a lead. He decides to start with the friend's description of Sirhan's sensitivity and tribulations as a boy, then point out the paradox between this description and what we have before us now, an assassin with a sick, twisted mind. This is the gist of the summary he sends New York. Maybe, he thinks as he begins to write, something better will come out of the afternoon session. Lacey Fosburgh, the blonde and lovely colleague who is working with him on the trial, is in the heavily guarded courtroom and will let him know immediately if anything develops.

At 2:11, Robinson's phone in the press room rings. It's Lacey.

"Sirhan just exploded," she says calmly. "Demanded his own execution. Said he was being railroaded. Fired his attorneys. Demanded to plead guilty to all charges and admitted he killed Senator Kennedy after twenty years of malice aforethought. The judge denied all requests. Said he'd put Sirhan in face mask and chains if he's not quiet. Whew!"

Robinson tears to shreds what he has already written. He takes down Lacey's words on the typewriter. She has it all, down to the quotation marks. "I'll call you back," she says. "The judge is calling the court back into session."

It's 5:15 in New York. Robinson calls Irv Horowitz. "Kill my summary," he tells him and fills him in on the courtroom drama.

Horowitz passes the word to Gene Roberts. Roberts reports it immediately to Abe Rosenthal and the bullpen editors who are reading through the stacks of summaries provided by each news desk to determine candidates for page 1. The Sirhan story has become a candidate.

Roberts, Horowitz and Butsikares go over their list of stories and decide which, besides "Ike," they will place in the page 1 sweepstakes. The Washington bureau's schedule is still flexible. During the afternoon David Jones, on the Washington news desk, has sent in additions and deletions to the list he filed at noon. He has added a story slugged "Lawyer," to be written by Fred Graham. "Exclusive," he wired the desk. "Alabama lawyer who represented Klansman is opposed for U.S. Attorney appointment by Postmaster General Blount."

The "Lawyer" story actually turned out to be the kind that

comes on strong and fades as you get into it. Graham, who covers the Supreme Court and the Justice Department, had planned to spend today, Friday, at the Court, briefing himself on the decisions the Court was scheduled to hand down the following Monday. When he stopped by the bureau to pick up his mail, he found a memo passing along a tip from The Times's stringer in Montgomery, Alabama.

The stringer had called to suggest that The Times might want to dig into a local story that the liberal forces in Montgomery had a candidate for U.S. Attorney named Ira De-Ment, who had been unanimously endorsed by the Alabama Republican patronage committee, but that Postmaster General Blount was pushing an old friend of his for the job and was leaking the fact that DeMent had once represented the Ku Klux Klan. The implication was that DeMent, who had also represented a Black Muslim, was more liberal than Blount's man.

Those were the facts in the memo that greeted Graham. He sat down at his desk and made a few phone calls. He learned that DeMent was a liberal who had defended a Klansman as a matter of duty and was now being punished for it. Graham told this to Bob Phelps, the bureau news editor. They agreed that it sounded like a good story. It was then that Jones scheduled it to New York.

But as Graham got deeper into it, the story faded in a way that changed its whole cast. He was tempted to dump it, or to needle it a bit to make it come out as clear-cut and newsworthy as it had at first appeared. But he resisted the temptation.

It seemed that Blount apparently did not tip off the Justice Department about DeMent's KKK representation. The FBI discovered it when they ran a check on him. Also, DeMent did not defend a Klansman. He represented the Klan for a fee in a civil action brought by the Government, and he seemed to think nothing of it. Graham realized that this was not the idealistic small-town lawyer who defends any and all needy defendants. It was a guy who didn't see anything unusual in taking the Klan's money to represent it against a Government suit to enjoin the Klan from burning crosses and shooting guns in the night. There was enough to justify a story, but not enough to make a really good one. Graham wrote it without much enthusiasm. When he saw it in The Times next morning, he thought: "They put it where it belongs. On the obituary page."

• • •

As dusk settles over Washington, reporters return to the bureau from Capitol Hill, from the Pentagon and from all the other Government agencies that generate news. They report to David Jones, tell him what they've got, get their space allotments and begin to write.

Eileen Shanahan, back at her desk after sitting through a Senate Ways and Means Committee hearing on taxes, flips through her notes and decides there really isn't much there. She tells Jones. He notifies New York: "Scratch taxes. Use wire short if desired."

William Blair tells Jones that Secretary of the Interior Hickel's appearance before the Senate Public Works Committee is a better story than he had anticipated. Hickel called for tougher laws to protect off-shore water from pollution, surprising testimony from the Cabinet member whose confirmation by the Senate had been delayed because he was suspected of showing too much sympathy to the oil interests.

Jones calls the national desk. "Blair's 'Leak' story is a possibility for page 1," he tells Horowitz and cues him in on the Secretary's unexpectedly tough stand against pollution.

William Beecher, home from the Pentagon and at work on his antimissile story for Sunday's paper, is interrupted by a call from the national copydesk in New York. They want further cuts in a story he filed earlier in the week, also for Sunday's paper, on outgoing Air Force Secretary Dr. Harold

Brown. Beecher had already cut the 8,500-word interview, which he had recorded on tape, down to 1,400 words. Now New York wants it cut in half. Beecher reluctantly agrees to the suggested deletions. He has no alternative. A reporter can fight to preserve his story, but the final decision rests with the editors in New York. Beecher was not sorry, when he saw Sunday's paper, to discover that the story ran without his by-line.

John Finney, back from the State Department, tells Jones that the Russian position in the communications satellite negotiations, though ambiguous, seems to be similar to the United States position—in favor, that is, of a single global space communications system. He'll write a story to that effect.

"What's the slug?" he asks Jones.

"Intelsat," Jones tells him.

As Finney sits down at his typewriter and writes the identifying word "Intelsat" at the top of the page, Eileen Shanahan, at a neighboring desk, erupts in a sulfurous argument with Jones.

Jones has approached her with a query from New York about her story yesterday on the tax hearings. Abe Rosenthal wants to know how come, as the New York *Daily News* reported and she had not, John D. Rockefeller III could have arranged his charitable contributions in such a way as to pay no taxes at all?

This query, which came out of the editors' meeting in New York this morning, sets Shanahan seething. She tells Jones that Rockefeller said he *could* do this, but didn't; that this particular tax gimmick has been described repeatedly in *The New York Times,* but if New York wants it she supposes she can write it again. Jones asks her to give him a memo to that effect. She bangs it out. He tones it down and transmits it to New York.

• • •

Edwin L. Dale, Jr., and Eileen Shanahan share the economics beat in the Washington bureau. Most of their stories appear on the financial-business news pages, and they are on the phone several times a day exchanging story ideas with Thomas Mullaney, the financial-business news editor. Mullaney passes on requests and suggestions from the home office; Dale and Shanahan counter with ideas and suggestions of their own. Unless they are writing on a subject that has obvious political connotations—such as an economic policy statement at a Presidential press conference—their copy is handled by the financial-business news department rather than by the national desk. "Fin-biz," the department's abbreviated moniker, is, like Sports, an independent and self-contained news operation. It has its own staff of sixty-five editors, reporters, copyreaders and statisticians. It gets more space in the paper, day in and day out, than any other news subdivision, starting off with a fixed daily allotment of thirty-six columns for market tables.

Mullaney competes just as keenly for page 1 space as any other editor. Earlier this afternoon he advised Lewis Jordan that he had two possibilities: one, a piece by Herbert Koshetz on the recent dramatic reduction of thefts in New York City's garment area; the other, a story on why the price of conglomerate stocks plunged during the day. The Stock Exchange president's statement that the Big Board was considering delisting the shares of two conglomerates might be the only reason. But, Mullaney told Jordan, Shanahan was checking out an Associated Press report that the tumble was triggered by a speech in Illinois by the new antitrust chief, Richard W. McLaren, in which he threatened to bring suit against conglomerate mergers.

Shanahan and Mullaney suspect that the A.P. reporter in Illinois, probably not too tuned in on the antitrust laws, might have gotten the fine points wrong. But it's worth looking into. Shanahan calls a contact at the Justice Department.

It is as she thought. McLaren actually said nothing more than he had said earlier to a Senate Judiciary Committee when it had questioned him before confirming his appointment.

"It's good for a short spread," she tells Mullaney, "but he didn't say anything we haven't reported before."

Mullaney withdraws "conglomerates" as a front-page candidate. It will run, instead, on the first financial page, twinned (under a common head) with a story written in New York on the Stock Exchange president's statement.

• • •

Conglomerates are also on Vartanig Vartan's mind as he returns to Fin-biz after lunch to prepare to write the day's stock-market lead. He spent the morning where the action is, in the financial district in downtown Manhattan. In early afternoon he watched the Dow-Jones news ticker, the stock tape and the "Quotron" machines that provide him with instantaneous market reports from teleprinters at desk side. Peter Elkovich, a statistician who sits beside him, has monitored the stock and news tickers through the day, correlating price changes with what has caused the activity.

Vartan mulls over his lead. Popular stock averages are slightly higher, but conglomerate stocks are hard hit. He decides this will be the point to stress. Big-name conglomerates have wobbled down to new lows.

He scans the market stories coming in thick and fast from the wire-service printers and the wrap-up data on the market as it begins to flow from the news service and Dow-Jones tickers. This is fill-in information on the most active stocks, new highs and lows, advancing and declining issues. Spotting a stock that has made a sizable price change for no apparent reason, he calls industry analysts on Wall Street to see if they know anything about it.

He calls the New York Stock Exchange to check on block activity—blocks of 10,000 or more shares trading on the market. Only thirty-five blocks appeared on the tape today, against fifty-four yesterday. This means that activity by institutions such as mutual funds and pension funds is going on at sharply reduced levels. Everybody is cautious about the market. Big Board volume continues low—less than 9 million shares.

It's time to put his findings onto paper. "The stock market turned in an uneven performance yesterday . . .", he writes, and grinds out a column and a half (about 1,100 words) to run as the lead financial story under the heading "Stock Drop Hits Conglomerates."

At 5:25 he's finished. He turns his copy in to Lee Kanner, Mullaney's assistant in charge of copy and the layout of financial's first, or "dress," page. Kanner scans it and passes it to the copydesk, which is now moving copy rapidly to the composing room.

As it must.

                            • • •

Fin-biz copy has first priority in the composing room at this hour. All of it must be off the typesetting machines by 7 o'clock to clear the decks for the last big rush of general news. Tonight, financial and business news will fill sixty columns— seven and a half pages—including four and a half pages of market tables. These pages will be among the first to close— the first to be completed—along with the editorial page, the women's page and the split page. The flow of pages from the composing room to the stereotype shop, where plates for the rotary presses are molded, must be smooth and steady to avoid jam-ups hard on edition time.

Rosenthal has approved the layout for the women's page, which has been prepared in the women's news department. He has okayed the split page, dominated tonight by the picture layout of Les Halles, the Paris market. The editorial page is the only page in the paper that does not fall in the news department's ken. It is wholly the product of the editorial board, from conception until it appears in the printed paper.* This is not just happenstance. It's in The Times's tradition of complete separation of news and opinion.

All the other pages—except for page 1, the financial front and the sports pages—are laid out by the news make-up editors. These men have before them, on their large rectangular desk in the newsroom, summaries of all stories, the length allotted for each and a list of illustrations that will be forthcoming from the picture desk. They indicate the placement of type and pictures on a duplicate set of page scratches provided by the advertising department. On each scratch, or dummy, the space to be filled by advertising has been blocked out.

The news is not shoveled haphazardly into the pages. It is organized, page by page, to assist the reader. The same sequence is maintained day after day—foreign news in the front pages, followed by national and local. Certain features are anchored in fixed position. Book news and the crossword puzzle are always on the page preceding editorials. The "News Summary and Index" appears on the first page of the second section. The financial and business pages are always in the second section. Television and radio programs and news are always on the next to the last page, preceded by the weather report, which in turn is preceded by the classified ads. Certain news categories float, but they don't float far. They remain roughly in the same part of the paper from day to day. The sports pages usually appear in the second section; cultural news, women's news and society are midway in the paper, though not in a fixed spot.

The advertising department has prepared its dummies in full knowledge of the page sequence. Publishers' ads have been scratched in on the book page, financial ads on the financial pages, sporting goods ads on the sports pages. The adver-

---

* The Op-Ed page, the page facing the editorial page, now also falls under the jurisdiction of the editorial page editor.

tising department has also kept the news department's open space requests in mind. Foreign news, for example, will run through page 14 tonight, and pages 2 and 3 have been left relatively free of advertising. These will be display pages, spots where foreign news can be displayed with attractive layouts.

David Lidman, the chief make-up editor, distributes the scratch sheets to his assistants. One man takes the early-closing pages—financial and business, obituaries, ships, TV, culture. Another takes national and local news pages. Lidman himself places the news on the foreign pages. On the open space on page 3, for example, he scrawls "Nixon," blocks out areas for photos of Nixon in Paris and indicates that the remaining space will be filled with Nixon copy jumped from page 1.

When the make-up editors complete the jigsawlike placement of stories and illustrations, they send the scratch sheets to the composing room to guide the printers as they make up the pages. The make-up editors themselves follow their dummies to the composing room to direct the placement of type in the page forms. Lidman serves, in effect, as the newsroom's liaison with the printers, making sure that the copy flow from the typesetting machines to the page forms holds steady through the evening so that pages can close on schedule.

. . .

Rosenthal and the bullpen editors—Ted Bernstein, Lewis Jordan and Larry Hauck—have read the summaries of the principal stories provided by each news desk, sizing up and appraising the whole news picture. Each man, independently, has listed those stories he thinks merit front-page display.

At 5:30, they meet with the foreign, national and metropolitan editors to get a final rundown on late-breaking stories and to probe more searchingly into the specific content of important stories. There is always stiff competition among the news desks for front-page position, and editors argue determinedly for their favorite stories.

Tonight, Arthur Gelb makes a pitch for the school story—forty cops in one school maintaining order. Racial tensions exacerbated by the recent teachers' strike.

"I don't think it's too much," Rosenthal comments. Hauck agrees. "Putting it outside indicates that something really big is going on."

Seymour Topping knows that tonight foreign news is in the enviable position of dominating the front page. He can afford to be generous. If space is tight, he volunteers to withdraw one of his recommendations—a dispatch from Prague on the Czechoslovakia Communist Party's rejection of blind obedience to Moscow.

They review the plans for handling the Eisenhower obituary, should the former President die. "Felix Belair just called from Washington," Gene Roberts reports. "He assures us Ike will live through the night." This is not so fey as it sounds. They all know that Belair is getting his information firsthand from Eisenhower's doctors, not simply from routine news bulletins.

The picture editor presents his page 1 offerings. Not too much tonight. There are wirephotos from Paris of Nixon and de Gaulle. There's nothing on the confrontation in the schools. "The story's not visual," was the report of the staff photographer who went from one trouble area to another trying for pictures.

The meeting breaks up a few minutes after six. Topping, Roberts and Gelb return to their newsroom desks. Copy is moving to the composing room, but the flow is not so steady as it should be. Walter Mattson, the production director, asks that it be speeded up. A slow trickle now, he knows, means a flood at edition time. The call goes out over the metropolitan desk loud-speaker:

"We need copy in short takes."

Abe Rosenthal and the bullpen editors concentrate now on the make-up of page 1. They are completely on top of the news picture as of this hour.

Page 1 is the newspaper's showcase. The best stories are selected for it—and "best" can mean the most important, or the most readable, or the most unusual. The Times believes that a newspaper's principal purpose is to inform, so its editors put most emphasis on the important, though they are always on the lookout for the other qualities. The best front page, to them, is one that has something of everything.

To give a sense of organization to the essentially chaotic news of the day, stories on page 1 are grouped according to subject matter, and their importance in relation to each other is indicated by their position on the page and the size of their headlines. When the news is sensational, the treatment is bold, with large, occasionally page-wide, heads. On normal nights the display is more conservative and is often confined to one-column heads.

A dummy—a piece of paper ruled into eight columns to simulate a newspaper page—lies on the table in front of the editors as they start to lay out page 1. They indicate the position of each story by marking on the dummy the identifying word, or slug, that has been assigned to it. They indicate the type of headline over each story by a single letter of the alphabet, or by a combination of a letter and number. These letters and numbers are keyed to a chart that contains all possible typographical patterns used in Times headlines.

Headline types and styles are not created at the whim of an editor. A newspaper settles on a certain family of headline type and consistently sticks with this family—in various sizes and design—to maintain its identity, its continuity of appearance.

The lead, or most important, story is placed in column eight, the right-hand column. The off-lead, or second in importance, goes in column one, the left-hand column.

"Well, what's the best story?" Bernstein asks.

Somebody suggests Nixon.

"Nixon is making the paper look the same every night," Rosenthal comments. For the past week the President's tour has, in fact, dominated the front page.

Tonight, though, there's not much meat in the Nixon story. They decide to lead, instead, with the Berlin crisis and make Nixon the off-lead, each story to be topped with an A (one-column) head. So it's foreign news on the right, foreign news on the left. What other foreign news is available to link the outside columns and thus maintain the grouping of stories in similar fields? A picture of Nixon and de Gaulle is selected to fill the top of columns two, three, four and five. The war lead from Vietnam is placed in column six and, in column seven, under a small X-head, a story, still to come, from Ben Welles in Washington on the State Department's reaction to the Soviet threat to Berlin.

They move down the page. They decide to play the three most important national stories under the four-column Nixon photo. There's "Ike," for sure, and "Sirhan." What will be the third? They settle on "Intelsat." One of the three will carry a two-column R-head. The others will run on either side of it with single-column heads.

Jordan suggests that "Sirhan" get the big play, the center position.

"But we had more or less the same story a few days ago," Rosenthal points out, "though that time he exploded in chambers instead of in open court."

They decide to give the play to "Ike."

They work their way down the page. A few more foreign stories are scratched in on the right side—"Czech," "Dutch" (Roman Catholic bishops in the Netherlands approve role for married priests), "Zurich" (Swiss protest to three Arab nations over machine gunning of an El Al airliner at the Zurich airport). Two local stories dominate the lower left side of the page—"Census," by Peter Kihss; and "Garment," by Herbert Koshetz. The bottom left-hand corner is still empty. They settle on "Dues," Seth King's story on the agency shop for municipal employes.

"That's it," Bernstein says as he checks the dummy. Thirteen stories, the average number. No startling news, and they have not tried to sensationalize it by typographical fireworks. It's a conservative front page.

The page 1 dummy is run through a copying machine. Duplicates are distributed to every editor's desk, to the composing room, to the writer who is preparing the summary for the split page, and to The Times News Service.

The News Service, busily transmitting the day's news file to its 300 newspaper and magazine clients around the world, puts a "For Your Information" bulletin on its wire: THE N.Y. TIMES 1st EDITION DUMMY PAGE 1 FOR SATURDAY, MARCH 1 . . ." and lists the stories, indicating their position on the page with "TOPS," "FOLD," "BOTTOM."

· · ·

Half an hour after the page is laid out on 43d Street, its content is known in the London, Paris, Tokyo and Washington bureaus of The Times, all of which receive the News Service wire.

In Paris, where it's past midnight, the fronting chatters in as the last takes of Bob Semple's story are delivered to the bureau by messenger from the Hotel Georges Cinq, for transmission to New York.

The Paris bureau is approaching the end of a long day. Max Frankel and Henry Tanner, after a leisurely dinner, are tying up the loose ends of the Nixon story. Frankel has finally reached Robert McCloskey, Nixon's spokesman for the State Department, and has tried to get something from him on the United States reaction to the Berlin situation. When he hangs up the phone, he sends a message to Seymour Topping:

ON BERLIN, BELIEVE IT OR NOT MOST OF OUR HIGHEST RANKING TRAVELERS WENT TO BED AFTER DEGAULLE DINNER AND ONLY THE BRIEFEST FILL-IN AVAILABLE ON SOVIET NOTES. THERE IS NO FORMAL REACTION BUT EYEM SENDING YOU SEVERAL PARAGRAPHS BASED ON INFORMED OFFICIAL WHO SAID WASHINGTON HAD EXPECTED SOME STIFFENING AS SOON AS NIXON HAD BEEN THROUGH BERLIN. DIPLOMATIC ACTIVITY EXPECTED BUT NONE YET DISCLOSED HERE.

Frankel taps out the several paragraphs, drops them off in the wire room, lights up his ninety-fourth pipe of the day, says "Good night" and heads for his hotel. Tanner lingers. There may be further queries from New York, and besides he wants to make sure that the text of Nixon's toast at the de Gaulle dinner comes through. It does, by messenger, at 12:40 A.M. Tanner reads it. "Pretty poor Nixon," he thinks as he passes it to the wire room for transmission to New York.

The foreign desk shoots back a cabled query: ASSUME NIXON SPOKE IN ENGLISH, DEGAULLE IN FRENCH. Tanner replies: RIGHT.

Tanner instructs the overnight wire-room operator to give Frankel's hotel phone number to the London bureau. If the foreign desk has further questions, they will come through London, and the London bureau will, he hopes, call Frankel for the answers instead of him. It's almost 1 o'clock as he walks home in the cold, starless night through the Tuileries and across the Seine.

. . .

In the New York newsroom, work is fast and tense as deadline draws nearer. Every editor and every copyreader knows what must be done. All stories are heading for the composing room by pneumatic tube to be set in type. Early stories have already been set, and printers, working from the dummies provided by the make-up desk, are placing the type in its allotted space in the page forms. Other stories are sent up marked "hed to kum" or "lede to kum," notification to the composing room that the headline or the lead will come later, covering later developments.

The picture desk has cropped the four-column page 1 picture of Nixon and de Gaulle and has selected, from stacks of agency prints, other pictures of the tour for use on pages 2 and 3, where the Nixon jump, or continuation, and side stories will be displayed. Pictures of the Eshkol funeral, which Picture Editor John Morris ordered from a photographer in Jerusalem rather than rely on agency coverage, have arrived by radio via London. Staff photographers, back from city assignments, have developed their pictures in the photo lab adjacent to the picture desk and have dropped 8 by 10 prints on the picture editor's desk. The picture agencies to which The Times subscribes have delivered hundreds of prints covering significant events of the day wherever they occurred.

From this mass of material, forty-seven illustrations have been selected for tonight's paper. Picture deskmen crop them to the desired size, write captions, mark the size required and send the prints to the photoengraving department to be converted into metal engravings.

Copy is streaming in now over the high-speed transmitter

that links the Washington bureau with the 43d Street wire room. Clerks strip it from the machine and rush it to the national desk. Copyreaders, working against time, process it swiftly. They must shut off their regular run at 7:20 P.M.; everything sent to the composing room after that hour must be for page 1, which carries last-minute news and is the last page to close.

Douglas Robinson's story from Los Angeles on the Sirhan trial has come in on a Western Union printer. Robinson's copy does not usually reach New York until after 7 P.M., making for a race against time if it is to get into the first edition. But today the big news broke early in the day. By 3 o'clock Los Angeles time (6 o'clock in New York) he had filed his story of Sirhan's blowup. He lingered in the press room awaiting possible queries from New York and waiting for a call from Lacey Fosburgh in the courtroom with a fill-in on late developments. A few minutes after three the call came from Miss Fosburgh. "Here we go again," she reported. "The defense lawyers have offered to resign, and Sirhan's mother has gone on the stand. She's crying so hard the judge has recessed the court until Monday." Robinson takes notes, hangs up, writes inserts for his story and hands them to Western Union to file. It's 6:30 in New York when he calls Chick Butsikares on the night national desk and advises him that court has adjourned and inserts are on the wire. "Everything's in hand," Butsikares tells him, "and it will all make the first edition. No questions. Good night."

The sun is still piercing the Los Angeles smog when Robinson and Miss Fosburgh, relaxed at the prospect of a free week end ahead, sit down in the Palm Court of the Ambassador Hotel for a drink and a rehash of the day's events.

• • •

The metropolitan desk works against the same urgent deadline pressure as the national desk. Reporters must have their copy in by 7 o'clock unless they are working on front-page stories, in which case they have twenty minutes more leeway. The call, "Copy," comes from the far reaches of the newsroom as writers, working against the clock, pull the pages from their typewriters and summon copyboys to run them to the desk for processing.

At 6:10, Sheldon Binn warns through the loud-speaker: "Fifty minutes to go."

"We're over our space allotment," Binn informs Gelb. Together they run through the schedule. Here's one that can go into the culture department quota—Henry Raymont's story on the acquisition by Time Inc. of twenty-two suburban weeklies in Chicago. Others will be combined or knocked down to short spreads. Still others, if not urgent hard news, will be held over until Sunday's paper, when, traditionally, there is less news and more space.

As stories reach the desk, George Barrett, who has read the summaries and knows what their structure should be, skims them and passes them to the adjacent copydesk to be readied for the composing room. If he thinks the story doesn't come off, he tosses it to Binn, who takes it up with Gelb, and the reporter may be asked to redo it.

The same procedure for handling copy is followed on the foreign and national desks, but the metropolitan editor is the only one of the three who faces his men head on. The foreign and national editors relay their ideas, requests and complaints by cable or telephone. The metropolitan editor confronts his staff eyeball to eyeball. There is no buffer to tone down reactions, to protect him from snarls and gripes. But Gelb likes it that way.

"The daily confrontation adds excitement to the job," he says. "When a reporter comes up and suggests a good idea for a story, there is an electric reaction between us. He adds something. I add something. And from this give-and-take can evolve something very creative."

The pressure on the foreign desk has lifted somewhat. Most of its stories have cleared the copydesk and are on the composing-room typesetting machines. They have been trimmed or revised if necessary, and in the Nixon story shorts from Paris have been incorporated into Semple's over-all lead. Now the desk is polishing, honing, cleaning up. Cables bounce back and forth across the Atlantic.

A message goes out to Robert Doty, Rome bureau chief, who has filed a wrap-up of the effect on Italy of Nixon's visit and, by midnight, thought he was clear. Gerald Gold asks him: CAN YOU SEND OBIT ON GUSTAVO CARDINAL TESTA WHO DIED AT VATICAN RESIDENCE TODAY? Doty can, and does—a half-column within an hour.

Gold gets off a query marked "Urgent" to David Binder in Berlin: DOES WORD "TRUCK" REFER LITERALLY TO TRUCKS OR ALSO COVER AIR AND WATER CARRIAGE OF INDUSTRIAL GOODS?

Binder, who has had a long day, replies somewhat testily: 99% OF WEST GERMAN INDUSTRIAL GOODS ARE SHIPPED BY TRUCK OR, IF YOU WILL, TRAILER TRUCK. UNURGENTLY YOURS, AS WE SAY IN THIS LAND OF CALM.

Binder sends this reply through the London bureau wire room and informs the bureau operator that he is closing the Berlin office and will be reachable at the Hotel Kempinski. The London operator tells him, on telex: "I thought you might want to see this one before you leave," and relays a message just received from Topping in New York. It says: YOUR FINE BERLIN WRAPUP LEADING PAPER.

Still missing from the foreign desk file is Ben Welles's story, scheduled for page 1, on State Department reaction to the Soviet note. Though the Washington bureau falls under the direction of the national news desk, when its stories concern foreign affairs, as Welles's does today, they come under foreign-desk jurisdiction and are counted in the foreign-desk quota.

Welles has tried all afternoon without success to reach Carl Bartch, the State Department spokesman. At 6:45 he is still waiting for Bartch to call him. His phone rings. It's Bartch's secretary. Hold on, she tells him, for Mr. Bartch. He waits, and waits, and waits. At last Bartch comes on, very faintly, and begins: "I have a long statement in three parts describing the meeting this afternoon between the Acting Secretary of State, Mr. Richardson, and the Soviet Ambassador, Mr. Dobrynin. . . ." Mr. Bartch is talking on a "conference line" which is hooked into the telephones of half a dozen reporters from different news media. Welles puts on the headset attached to his desk telephone and takes the statement on his typewriter. It's long, as Mr. Bartch promised, and, Welles thinks when he has it all down, "nothing more than an extended version of what I told Gold this afternoon would come from State." He knocks it down to a 600-word story: "The United States warned the Soviet Union today about what appeared to be a mounting campaign by Russia and East Germany to bar access to West Berlin. . . ."

Less than an hour later, Welles, his morning malaise apparently forgotten, is winding up the day at the Brazilian Embassy, where he has scheduled a quiet chat with the Brazilian Ambassador. He is called to the Embassy phone. It's David Rosenbaum, the night deskman in the bureau.

"Sorry to bother you, Ben," Rosenbaum apologizes, "but New York doesn't think the word 'warn' in the lead of your story is justified. Can you give them an insert explaining what is meant by 'warn'?"

Welles explodes. He tells Rosenbaum what he can tell the editors in New York about what they don't know about the English language. "I wrote 'warn,' and goddamn it I mean 'warn.'

Nobody in his right mind could read it any other way."

Rosenbaum passes on an edited version of Welles's reaction to Gerald Gold, who had questioned "warn" in the first place. Gold still believes it is the wrong word; it implies retaliation, and there is no hint in Welles's story of U.S. retaliation against the Soviets.

If Welles doesn't want to change it, Gold will—and does— for he is the man who will be held responsible for what shows up in the paper. The story, as it appeared at the top of page 1, began: "The United States expressed its concern to the Soviet Union today . . ."

• • •

In the composing room, copy sent by pneumatic tube from the newsroom is piling up on the copy cutters' desk. There it is scissored into takes—fragments of a few lines to a paragraph or two—and each take is given a number and letter to facilitate assembly of finished type in proper order.

The takes are passed out to operators to be set in type. The Times uses two typesetting systems: linotype, the familiar manual line-casting system; and teletypesetting (TTS), an electronic system. Linotype operators tap out the characters in the copy on a keyboard somewhat like a typewriter, and the machines automatically measure out column widths and cast each line in molten metal, which hardens quickly into cold type. Operators at TTS machines, which are also equipped with typewriterlike keyboards, punch copy onto coded tape. The tape is fed into electronic line-casting machines which, without benefit of operator, produce molten metal lines.

When the type comes out of the line-casting machines it is carried to the so-called "dump bank," where each take is dropped into position in a metal tray, called a galley. The number or letter on each take of type determines its position in the galley. Headlines, set on other machines, are fitted into their proper galleys.

The assembled galley of type goes to the proof presses, where proofs are pulled for editors and proofreaders. The type is now ready for insertion in the page form.

Advertising copy goes through practically the same routine, only earlier. Copy for display ads, sent to the composing room by carrier from the advertising department two floors below, is dropped on the mark-up desk, where it is marked for composition and distributed to the typesetting machines. The various parts of the ads, including cuts sent down from the photoengraving department, are assembled on the make-up banks, where printers, using the original copy as a guide, collate type and cuts into the finished ad.

Just before 5 o'clock the ads were moved on metal-wheeled tables to the page forms on the other side of the composing room. By 6:35, when the news dummies are distributed, the ads must be in position in the forms.

News and advertising meet for the first time as galleys of type are carried from the proof presses to the page forms. Printers check the type against their dummies and begin to place it in the space allotted to it.

Though there are still gaping holes in the black metal page forms, the pages that will be the first to close are beginning to fill. Make-up editors for the women's page and the editorial page are at the stones, directing the printers in the placement of type.

The women's page is featuring tonight a layout of African-inspired fashions. Early in the afternoon Joan Whitman, assistant women's news editor, was informed by the publication office that the page would be free of ads. This meant that the department, which dummies its own page, had plenty of room to display its exotic pictures of turbans, togas and trousers as a frame for the story written by Angela Taylor. Miss Taylor is one of twelve women's news reporters who cover fashion, food, family news, home furnishings and other news of particular interest to women. The lone male writer in this women's page is Food Editor Craig Claiborne. The department also calls upon general assignment reporters for special stories for its page. Tonight, for example, Nan Robertson of the Washington bureau has a piece on an industrial design show at the Smithsonian Institution. Since space is not a problem, her story will be illustrated with a dramatic half-page-deep picture of one of the exhibits. The bottom of the page features coffee-cake recipes by Jean Hewitt, the home economist.

Mrs. Hewitt prepared these recipes in the test kitchen several days ago and put the pudding to the proof by using the ladies of women's news as tasters. She frequently adds their judgment to her own. The Viennese tortes that she put together this morning ended up as afternoon snacks in the department today. When Harrison Salisbury, assistant managing editor who neither drinks nor smokes but whose sweet tooth is finely honed, got wind of the tasting session, he dropped everything to join the ladies. His verdict: "Wunderbar."

The women's news editor, Charlotte Curtis, is in the field today, as she frequently is, writing about fashionable people. She is in Palm Beach gathering material for one of her irreverent chronicles of life among the upper crust. She and Robert Walker, a Times photographer, have spent the warm, sunny day cruising in their rented Hertz car from one social event to the next. Walker's camera has caught the smart set at tennis, aboard their yachts, in their beach houses. Miss Curtis has caught their conversation and jotted it all down in her ever-ready notebook.

She has noted that Mrs. Woolworth Donahue started her tennis morning by saying hello to Diablo (a harlequin Great Dane with one blue eye and one brown eye), removing her engagement ring ("a diamond almost as big and heavy as her tennis racket") and turning on the hi-fi, which sends the sounds of "If I Were A Rich Man" out over the court.

At the Joseph Neffs' palatial seaside villa, the living room was so large that it took Miss Curtis a few minutes to decide which of nearly twenty chairs and sofas to sit on. Into her notebook she scribbled Mrs. Neff's comment: "Wearing an evening dress twice in a row is a bore for your friends."

This afternoon, however, Miss Curtis lost a bit of her usual aplomb because of a slight accident that on any other beat a reporter would take in stride. During a hamburger luncheon aboard a yacht she spilled a big glob of catchup on her pink, sleeveless dress. There has been no time between social events to get back to the hotel to change. The beautiful people have tried to help remove the spot, but it's stubborn. It makes her a little uncomfortable.

· · ·

In the composing room, as 7 o'clock nears, half of the type is in position in the editorial page. The "Letters to the Editor" are in place and, above them, a "Topics" column by the novelist Philip Roth. "Topics" columns—essays by nonstaff writers pegged to events in the news—are a Saturday feature of the page.* Herbert Mitgang of the editorial board is charged with filling the space.

The Roth piece, titled "Reflections on the Death of a Library," has been several weeks a-borning. Mitgang, always on the lookout for "Topics" about urban or suburban New York, finds this is difficult material to get from writers. A month ago, when Roth's novel, *Portnoy's Complaint,* burst upon the literary market place, Mitgang wrote and asked him to do a piece about Newark, where he grew up. Roth replied that he didn't have anything particularly new to say about Newark but that he would keep the request in mind if a thought occurred.

Author and subject found each other this week. There was a report that the Newark Public Library would close for lack of funds. Roth called to say he would like to do a "Topics" column on this library, where he had spent so much of his

* Pieces like this now appear on the Op-Ed page.

youth. Mitgang told him to go ahead; he would schedule it for Saturday.

The copy came in a few days ago, and on its heels came a call from Roth. "What do you think of it?" he asked Mitgang.

"It's strong enough to save the Newark Public Library from closing, if words can do so," Mitgang told him.

Then they got down to specifics. Mitgang tried to get Roth to break up his long, book-style paragraphs, pointing out that they would be difficult to read in a news column, which is slightly under two inches in width. But Roth wanted them long, and that's the way they ran. When John Oakes was informed that the piece was scheduled, he sent back word from his hospital room: "I hope there are no four-letter words in it." There weren't.

Just before 7 o'clock, A. H. Raskin, acting today as editorial board chief, finishes the final reading of the editorials that will occupy the left-hand side of the page and turns them over to Robert Barzilay, the editorial-page make-up man. Barzilay nurses the page through the composing room and keeps an eye on late developments in the news that might affect editorials in the page. He will get in touch with Raskin at his home if such an emergency arises during the night.

The lead editorial, to be called "That Vietnam 'Understanding,'" will run 9½ inches, about half a column. It will be followed by one urging the Government, the medical profession and the pharmaceutical industry to combine to make an experimental drug called L-Dopa, a promising new treatment for Parkinson's disease, more available, under strict professional control. Both this editorial and the one that follows it, "Hickel vs. the Polluters," were written by Harry Schwartz, who today switched from his usual role as Kremlinologist-in-residence. In recent weeks the editorial page has been sharply critical of the Secretary of the Interior for his fumbling of pollution problems, but on the basis of his tough new position tonight's editorial commends him as "a quick learner—to the country's benefit."

Also on Raskin's schedule is an editorial by Harvey Segal, the board's economics specialist, on Administration plans to regulate one-bank holding companies. This is already in type, as editorials frequently are, and Mr. Segal has checked it out during the day. The final piece on the page will be Herbert Mitgang's "Mafia Bagels, Yet?"

The selection maintains the balance that John Oakes tries for on every editorial page—comments on international affairs, national affairs and state or local affairs, reflecting the three major divisions of Times news coverage.

Raskin has also given Barzilay an alternate schedule that calls for replating the editorial columns should Eisenhower die during the night. In that event, an editorial on Eisenhower will run across the top of both columns and underneath it the Hickel, banking and Parkinson cure pieces. The others will be jettisoned.

The Eisenhower editorial has been in type for some time. This afternoon Raskin updated it to take note of the General's indomitable will to live as reflected in his long illness.

A hitch has developed in the plans to increase the paper by four pages should Eisenhower die in time to get the full obituary in the midnight edition. The production department has informed Ray Nelan of the publication office that it will be mechanically impossible to realign the press units in the brief time between editions and still maintain sufficient production.

The alternative is to clear four of the sixty-four scheduled pages. Nelan is in the composing room now, scratching out substitute advertising dummies, indicating which pages should be cleared for the obituary, which ads should be stripped, which repositioned. He is guided in his judgment by the advertising executives, who have indicated which ads can be pulled with a minimum of inconvenience to advertisers.

Nelan hands his revised dummies to the composing-room foreman. "I hope you won't have to use them," he says. "There's a twenty-thousand-dollar revenue loss riding on them."

· · · · · · · · 7 p.m.

Lewis Jordan's phone rings. It is David Jones in Washington. He and Bob Phelps have read the fronting as it came into the bureau on the News Service wire. It is their opinion that Blair's "Leak" story is a better choice for page 1 than Finney's "Intelsat." Jordan says he will read the copy, which is now in the house. The decision to place "Intelsat" outside was based on the summaries.

Jordan reads both stories and agrees with the Washington editors. He scratches "Intelsat" from the front-page dummy and scribbles "Leak" in its place. Butsikares sends a message to the bureau: "We are using the 'Leak' story on page 1 in place of 'Intelsat.' " The bullpen clerk passes the word to all desks.

The Washington editors frequently argue for swapping their own front-page stories, and New York is always ready to listen. Capital newsmen are familiar with the nuances of Government, as only men on the spot can be, and they have a keen sense of what is, and what is not, important. They want to protect themselves and their readers from seeming to put too much emphasis on something, or not enough on something else. If the top editors in New York agree with the reasoning, as they do tonight, the change is made.

· · ·

First-edition copy is moving swiftly to the composing room. Most of the local reporters have gotten a "good night" nod from Sheldon Binn, the signal that their stories have gone through, there are no questions, and they can leave. Binn checks his schedule and glances up at the clock. 7:15, and the last two stories are under the copyreaders' pens. No sweat. The copy will be clear on time tonight.

It was after 6 o'clock before Barnard Collier streaked into the newsroom and reported on the events that led to the black-white school clash in Plainfield, New Jersey. "Last night there was a fistfight in front of the school between black and white students," he told Binn, "and a traffic cop who tried to break it up was injured. That's why they had the auditorium meeting this morning. One remark led to another, and the meeting dissolved into a fight. I wouldn't be surprised if there's more trouble tonight."

"Give me a column," Binn told him. The story is crossing the desk now, in takes. If there's trouble later in the evening, Robert Smith, who has called in to report that he is in Plainfield, will send inserts.

• • •

Seth King, up from City Hall, is buried in background clips on municipal unions and their past efforts to get an agency shop clause in their contracts. His desk is piled high with folders from the morgue, the vast repository where every article that appears in The Times is filed in subject and biographical folders. King has checked technical points with Damon Stetson, the local staff's chief labor reporter. He has become as familiar with a complicated subject as it is possible to become in a few hours, and he is now at his typewriter. Binn has asked him for a column and a half. At 7:15, King sends up his last take.

• • •

Larry Van Gelder has faced the same problem of familiarizing himself quickly with a subject on which he knows nothing:

the Mayor's ponderously titled Pre-Arraignment Processing Facility. He got most of his information through a long telephone interview with Burton Roberts, the Bronx District Attorney, an important man in the experiment. Mr. Roberts sounded weary and digressed frequently from conversation about the experiment to make jokes and relate some of his humorous remarks to the Mayor during the formal ceremonies surrounding the beginning of the program. Van Gelder, with one eye on the clock, steered him back to pertinent stuff and, before they hung up, suggested that Roberts refresh his spirits over the week end by reading *Portnoy's Complaint.*

Binn told Van Gelder to write three-quarters of a column and slug it "Arraign." As frequently happens when a writer is not too sure of his subject, it was more difficult to keep it short than let it run. Van Gelder went over three-quarters and the copydesk cut it back. Space is tight tonight.

Van Gelder is sending up inserts now on stories written by other reporters who have already gotten "Good night." Inserts are the bane of rewrite men and comprise about one-third of their work. From the rewrite man's viewpoint, the person who wrote the story in the first place should have known enough to put in the material that he, the rewrite man, is ultimately asked to provide. From the reporter's viewpoint, inserts generally cover picky little points that slow a story without really adding to it—a quirk to be expected of editors and copyreaders.

Binn has seen a proof sent down from the composing room of Martin Tolchin's story slugged "Lindsay" and has asked Van Gelder to write an insert explaining that the Board of Education and the Metropolitan Transportation Authority are really arms of the state rather than the city. "And while you're at it," Binn tells him, "check the number of commissioners Tolchin has attributed to the Transit Authority." Van Gelder calls the Transit Authority's public relations man. The number of commissioners is correct as Tolchin has it. He writes the insert, a substitute for one paragraph in the story, and turns it in at 7:25.

• • •

The national desk has cleared its copy for the first edition and braced itself for a new load later in the evening when reporters will file inserts and, in some cases, whole new stories on events still under way, such as the Clay Shaw trial in New Orleans and the *Pueblo* hearing in Coronado. The Washington file was light tonight, as it generally is on Fridays when most Government bureaus adjourn early for the week end. Details have been clarified through messages over the teletype line that links the bureau with the 43d Street wire room. Chick Butsikares on the New York end and David Rosenbaum in Washington use the wire like two men talking face to face.

"Re 'Intelsat,' " Butsikares asks, "is Telecommunications Union same as Intelsat?"

"No," Rosenbaum replies. "The Telecommunications Union is concerned with cooperation on technical matters such as frequencies."

Butsikares: "Last paragraph 'Intelsat,' is Intersputnik System a name or Finney's term?"

Rosenbaum: "Intersputnik is a name."

Butsikares: "Re 'Ike,' can you elucidate 'commedical intimates,' please?"

Rosenbaum: "The word should be 'nonmedical,' not 'commedical.' "

• • •

At 7:15 Bob Semple's copy is still trickling in to the foreign desk. It has been slowed by heavy traffic on the leased circuit that is carrying it from Paris to London to New York. Parts of it came in garbled so that the London bureau wire-room operator had to repunch it. It will be well past 7:30 before the story is finally cleared, although proofs of the first part of it are on Gerald Gold's desk before the end of it reaches New York.

This presents no urgent production problem. The 7:30 copy deadline has been established for just such emergencies. If the flow through the composing room holds smooth through early evening and copy is not permitted to pile up, a few late takes or inserts on important stories can reach the composing room as late as 9 o'clock and be processed in time to make the 9:15 closing.

Gold checks through wire-service copy from Paris to make sure Semple has all the angles covered. He spots an Associated Press report that the French Government's reaction to Nixon's visit was "cordial and productive." Nothing like that has yet appeared in Semple's story. Gold sends the A.P. copy to the composing room to be used as a shirttail —a follow-up story appended to the main article—on Semple should he not touch on the "cordial and productive" aspect. But as Semple's copy resumes, it is thorough in every respect. The A.P. short is ordered killed.

Al Siegal, who keeps the late watch on the foreign desk, is back now to pick up where he left off sixteen hours ago. Before Topping and Gold leave for the night, they brief him on what has taken place during those hours at the global command post on 43d Street and in bureaus around the world. They tell him which stories are the best, which are the weakest—information he must have in case he has to slash at the report later in the night to make way for new copy. Siegal briefs himself by reading the day's messages to correspondents. He takes particular note of requests for stories or inserts. This ensures that later on, when he adds or subtracts copy, he will be working in harmony, rather than at cross purposes, with the day editors.

To familiarize himself with the stories he will nurse through the night, Siegal reads through all the original copy and carefully checks Gold's list showing the prominence and the space allocated to each. A few points bother him as he reads: A

Russian Ambassador's name is misspelled; a diplomatic report is attributed to *The Washington Post* when it should be credited to *Newsday*. He's pretty sure the copyreaders have caught these slips by now, but he takes a few notes to be checked later against the first edition.

Topping and Gold turn over their desk to the nightside about 7:45. They were the first editors in, they are the first to leave, and their copy, because of the time difference, is generally the first to clear. Evan Jenkins, the assistant foreign editor who provides the overlap between dayside and nightside, will steer the foreign report through the first edition; then Siegal will take over.

• • •

Across the world in Vietnam, a new day has begun. As Seymour Topping boards a sweltering, overheated train for the ride to his home in Scarsdale, Terry Smith awakens in the sweltering Saigon heat. He has a busy few hours ahead. There is time this morning to update and freshen for late editions the story he filed last night for the first edition now going to press in New York.

At the Vietnam Press Center, Smith picks up the report of overnight developments issued by the Allied command: another fifteen shellings during the night, some more scattered fighting. The only thing that is clear is that American casualties are the target.

There is no morning briefing, as there is in the afternoon. Smith takes the mimeographed handouts to his office and puts in telephone calls to sources who can fill him in on details. It is as he thought: No pattern has yet developed in the offensive. His first-edition story can stand as is, with a few paragraphs added to include the night's fighting. He types them and carries them to the telegraph office. All he can do now is hope they get through to New York with a minimum of delay. Otherwise, he knows, the foreign desk will use agency copy.

The agencies have continuous communications, whereas the "specials"—the individual newspapers—have to wait their turn in the telegraph office.

. . .

As the hands of the newsroom clocks inch toward 8 o'clock, copyreaders lean back, light up, relax. The pressure is off. Except for bits and snippets and occasional inserts, first-edition copy is clear. The major decisions have been made. From now on it's a matter of following through on them.

Abe Rosenthal checks with the bullpen editors. Everything is smooth. "I'll be at home this evening," he tells them. Should there be a late news break involving a change in the front page, the bullpen will call him immediately, and he will take whatever action he deems necessary.

Arthur Gelb and Gene Roberts follow Rosenthal out of the newsroom, leaving their desks to their night men, who will notify them if anything unforeseen develops. Ted Bernstein goes out to dinner. He will return to the bullpen to check through the first edition for flaws when it streams from the presses less than two hours from now.

. . .

One floor above, in the composing room, the pressure is on. Printers in inky aprons bend over the chases like surgeons over the operating table. Working from page dummies and guided by make-up editors, they fit the pieces into place—ads, stories, headlines, illustrations.

The scoreboard under the composing-room clock, where Joe Hoard, a cigar-puffing printer's aide, posts the closing time of each page, shows ten pages closed. Two of them are full-page ads, four are classified ad pages, two are financial pages, two are cultural news.

"Let it go," the make-up editor instructs the printer when the last stick of type has been dropped into the page form. The printer locks the chase by screwing down pressure wedges, planes it with a mallet and hammer, and sticks a flag (a piece of metal) upright in the chase to signify that the page is closed—ready to be molded.

From this time on, until freshly printed copies leap from roaring presses, getting out the paper is a mechanical race against time.

Proof boys, alert for the appearance of the flag, slide the chase onto a metal truck and wheel it to the stereotype mat machines in a corner of the composing room. A mat—a heavy papier-mâché sheet—cut to the exact size of the page is laid over the metal frame, and a steel cylinder exerting a pressure of twelve tons is rolled over it, impressing each detail of the page on the mat. The page of type is then wheeled back to the bank on which it originally lay. It never leaves the composing room. It will be opened up for corrections and whatever other changes are called for during the night.

The mat, meanwhile, is dropped down a chute to the stereotype shop in the pressroom, five floors below the composing room. There the mat—the type side facing in—is curved to the shape of a cylindrical press roller and placed in an electric-powered plate-casting machine. A button is pressed, and the machine is in motion. A heavy steel cylinder moves to within one-half inch of the mat and clamps into place. Molten metal flows into the half-inch space over the mat's surface. The cylinder comes away, revealing a metal cast, an exact replica of the page in the composing room. With one difference. Now it is a single solid curved plate rather than separate pieces of flat type and engravings.

The plate-casting machines spew out finished plates at the rate of four a minute. Page numbers are painted on their surface in bold figures with black ink, and mechanical conveyors carry them along the concrete floor to the waiting presses.

The number of plates required for one night's press run is awesome. Tonight, twelve presses will run simultaneously to turn out the sixty-four page paper, each printing 40,000 complete papers an hour. Each must have an entire new set of page plates for each edition, because no single plate can hold up all night under the pressure of high-speed presses. In addition, pages must be rematted and recast every time a change is made in a page form in the composing room. Before the last press sighs to a stop at dawn tomorrow, the stereotypers will have cast more than 3,000 page plates.

. . .

A few minutes before 8 o'clock the first mats tumble down the chute from the composing room. Among the first to be locked into the plate-casting machines are the cultural news pages.

Art news runs heavy tonight, as it always does in the Saturday paper, and space for general amusement coverage—drama, dance, film and music—is at a premium. Art Critics John Canaday and Hilton Kramer, who tour the galleries early in the week, on Saturday discuss what they have seen. Their columns with illustrative material, and an antiques column by free-lance writer Marvin Schwartz, fill half the cultural news quota. Canaday's lead review is on the work of Grandma Moses; Kramer discusses the work of Lois Dodd; and each has brief comments on five or six other exhibits.

Don Forst, the cultural news editor, has featured on his display page, where two columns have been left clear of advertising, a piece by Critic-at-Large Howard Taubman on the Western Opera Association. Taubman, on a cultural swing of the West Coast, filed the story earlier in the week. It fits neatly into the space available tonight, and it doesn't require extensive illustration, an important consideration when space is tight. A single-column cut of the composer Gian-Carlo Menotti, whose work the company has been featuring, squares off the piece at the top of the page. Under it, Forst has tucked a review written by Richard F. Shepard of a French theater group's production of *Phedre*. He has also found room for a review from London of a campy musical, *Two Cities,* based on Dickens.

The rest of the first-edition cultural space is filled with theater, ballet and music reviews carried over from last night's late editions. These reviews are reprinted for readers across the country and around the world, most of whom see only the first edition. They will be replaced later in the evening by fresh reviews from critics who, at this hour, are setting out for halls all over town to attend performances in their respective fields.

It is impossible, of course, to cover every drama, dance, art exhibit and musical event that is presented. The critics, who work out the schedules for themselves and their staffs, try to cover the significant performances in major halls and off-off Broadway, in luxurious settings and in scruffy lofts, in New York, in Los Angeles, in Rome—wherever they are happening.

Today has been a lalapalooza for the denizens of Culture Gulch, the cultural news enclave at the north end of the newsroom. It is Vincent Canby's first day as film critic, as successor to Renata Adler. He had been informed of his elevation from number 2 critic to number 1 while on vacation on an isolated Caribbean Island. Arthur Gelb had called him from New York and, bucking atmospheric conditions, had with difficulty gotten the message to him: "You're the new film critic."

• • •

All day Canby has been swamped with telephone calls and buried under telegrams and letters from hundreds of friends —many of them, he notes cynically, rather newfound. Culture Gulch is a riot of flowers sent by the new critic's well-wishers, and on the ceiling floats a huge, helium-filled balloon, strung with streamers offering good luck in Yiddish, Chinese and Swahili.

In midafternoon, Canby broke from the high jinks to attend a screening of *The Prime of Miss Jean Brodie*. Now, locked in the glass cubicle behind which The Times stashes its stone-throwing critics, he is writing his review, which will appear two days from now, after the film's formal opening. Not a great film, is the gist of what he writes, but a great performance by Maggie Smith (who later won an Oscar for it)—and a happy way to start off on a tough job.

Clive Barnes is at City Center as the curtain rises on the Joffrey Ballet's revival of *Opus '65*. There is no theater opening tonight. Had there been, he would have taken whichever he considered more important and assigned the other to his assistant. Tonight is heavy on concerts, and music critics have fanned out to Carnegie Hall, Philharmonic Hall, the New York State Theater and Madison Square Garden.

• • •

The big event in sports is the Columbia-Princeton basketball game to nail down the Ivy League championship. Gordon S. White, Jr., has drawn the assignment, and Mike Lien, a staff photographer, will handle the picture detail. Lien will come back with action pictures to replace the space-holder that James Tuite, the assistant sports editor who is laying out the sports pages tonight, has ordered for the first edition—a three-column cut of the pole vaulter Bob Seagren, who will defend his title tomorrow at the Amateur Athletic Union indoor track and field championships in Philadelphia.

Now that night games have become such a big thing, many sports stories cannot be written in time for the first edition. The layout man, dummying the early pages, must be something of a clairvoyant. He has to know what is coming later, and he must be able to visualize what the pages will look like in the final edition. He will not get more space during the night; he must be prepared to throw out and cut back stories to make room for live copy. Frequently, the sports copydesk is just cranking up in late evening when the rest of the desks, except for an occasional late-breaking story, are all cleaned up.

Tonight, though, there is only college basketball, and stringers will file stories on games at Cornell, Brown and Yale. Tomorrow, the New York Knickerbockers will meet the

Boston Celtics at Madison Square Garden in their final encounter of the season. Lots of interest there, and worth an advance story tonight. The advance will ride through the first
edition, holding the space for late copy on tonight's games.

• • •

In the bullpen, Lewis Jordan and Larry Hauck are plowing
through proofs of stories sent down from the composing
room. They check the editing, the fairness and adequacy of
presentation, the clarity of the writing, the explanatory background, the effectiveness of the headlines. If they think there's
room for improvement, they take it up with the desk from
which the story emanated. They may question a story's accuracy, request that a certain point be amplied or clarified, or
ask that a headline be rewritten to bring out a different angle.
Once in a while they kill a story as trivial, or order a story cut
or lengthened if they consider it worth less or more space.
Most of their changes will make the first edition; others will
be inserted later in the night.

The bullpen's "In" basket is piled high with wire-service
copy chattering in from all earth's corners. If an important
story breaks suddenly, layouts will have to be shifted to get it
in the edition.

At 7:59, a United Press International bulletin is dropped
on Jordan's desk. It's from Beirut, Lebanon. It says: TRAV-
ELERS FROM DAMASCUS ARE REPORTING THAT
THE ARMY HAS OVERTHROWN THE SYRIAN GOV-
ERNMENT.

· · · · · · · · 8 p.m.

An immediate decision faces Lewis Jordan: rush into print with an indecisive fragment, or wait for confirmation?

Evan Jenkins hurries over from the foreign desk to confer with Jordan and Hauck in the bullpen. A coup in Syria would come as no great shock, they agree, for the country's ruling party has long been bitterly divided. But the U.P.I. bulletin is "iffy"; the other wire services have carried no word of a coup, nor has Dana Adams Schmidt, The Times's correspondent in Beirut, been heard from.

It's Jenkins's opinion that the situation is too tentative to use in the first edition. Jordan agrees.

"But let's get someone started on a Syrian backgrounder for the second edition if the story holds up," he tells Jenkins.

Jenkins asks Sheldon Binn for a rewrite man. Binn assigns Robert McFadden, who has just come in, one of the two late men on rewrite. Jenkins asks McFadden to study the clips on Syrian politics and start writing a background article to fill in the gaps in the readers' understanding if the coup report proves true.

Now to make contact with Schmidt.

It's 2:17 in the morning in London when a cable from Jenkins, marked "Urgent," reaches Jules Arbose, the bureau's dogwatch deskman. It's for relay to Schmidt. It says:

UNIPRESS REPORTS EXBEIRUT POLITICAL

SOURCES REPORT FROM DAMASCUS THAT SYRIAN ARMY UNDER DEFENSE MINISTER LT. GENERAL HAFEZ AL-ASSAD HAS OVERTHROWN THE REGIME OF PRESIDENT NOUREDDIN AL-ATASSI IN A BLOODLESS MILITARY COUP. AL-ATASSI RE- PORTED UNDER HOUSE ARREST. CAN YOU CON- FIRM AND FILE PLEASE?

Arbose dials the international telephone operator and learns that the London-Beirut circuit is closed for the night.

Maybe Paris can get through to Schmidt. He calls Jim Brown, the late deskman in the Paris bureau, and catches him as he is about to close the bureau for the night.

Brown tries to put through the call. He is told there will be a forty-five minute delay. He informs Arbose. Arbose cables Jenkins:

LONDON-BEIRUT PHONE LINES CLOSED DOWN. WE'VE PASSED MESSAGE TO PARIS DESK AND THEY HAVE CALL BOOKED TO SCHMIDT IN 45 MINUTES.

As Brown awaits the call to Beirut, the bureau's Reuters wire comes alive with its first report of a Syrian coup. He strips it from the machine.

· · ·

The insistent ring of the telephone shatters Dana Adams Schmidt's sleep in Beirut. He jumps out of bed and gropes his way, in the dark, to his office in another part of the house. He hopes to lift the receiver before the whole house comes alive; but he's too late. His wife awakens. His son stirs. His mother-in-law turns on the lights. The dog asks to go out. He squints at the clock. It's 4:10 A.M. (one hour later than Paris, seven hours later than New York).

Jim Brown comes on the line. He reads the message from Jenkins. "Reuters has a similar report, though somewhat more qualified," Brown says, and reads him the agency copy.

"I'll call you back," Schmidt says, "and let's hope this erratic radio-telephone will still be working."

He tiptoes from the phone in his office to the more sheltered living-room phone, hoping the family will go back to sleep while he gets busy waking people up.

He thinks he knows what it's all about. There were hints of trouble in Syria in the summary of the local press prepared for him this morning by his assistant, Ihsan Hijazi. And he had gotten further indications of Syrian unrest in a conversation this afternoon with a leading Lebanese information official.

He calls the local U.P.I. office. They have nothing more than has already gone on their wire. He calls the Reuters Beirut bureau and learns that the agency wrote its piece pretty much to keep up with U.P.I., though it does have a smattering of original information. He calls the French-language newspaper *L'Orient* and learns it is using the U.P.I. story and has nothing of its own. He awakens the editor of *Le Jour,* another French-language paper. The editor is helpful. Reuters's information, and the editor's, fit together.

Schmidt rouses his assistant, Hijazi, and reads him the agency bulletins. Hijazi has an elephantine memory. To the skeletonized facts that Schmidt has, he adds flesh and background pulled from some hidden storehouse in his mind.

A picture begins to emerge. Schmidt ruminates: U.P.I.'s lead is too hard. The point is that General al-Assad doesn't want power for its own sake but is insistent on uniting Syria and Iraq militarily against Israel. To that end, he wants to force the Syrian and Iraqi governments to come to terms. It is a power play, but not really a coup.

Schmidt thinks he has a pretty fair story. He jots down detailed notes, and he's ready to dictate. He puts in a call to the Paris bureau. It's a little after 5 A.M., still time to make the late editions in New York, if the call gets through. But it doesn't. It's maddening.

· · ·

In New York, all hands concentrate on getting the first edition to press. At 8:10, the composing-room scoreboard shows that nineteen of the sixty-four pages in tonight's paper have been locked up and wheeled away to the stereotype mat machines. At 8:20, twenty-one pages have gone. The minutes are flying; the closings are slow. Six pages should have gone between 8:10 and 8:20 if they are not to bunch up in the last minutes, choking the stereotype department and delaying the press run. Everyone is aware of it. Everyone pushes a little harder.

The bustling composing-room floor looks like utter chaos —but isn't. Beneath the surface excitement, men move with purpose and quiet deliberation.

The forty-three page forms still open have yawning holes. Type is scattered in galleys all over the room, coming hot from the line-casting machines. Here is the type of a story without its head. There is the head of a story without the type. Other stories await takes, or inserts, to complete them. Boys run proofs to the editors and to the proofroom.

After proofs are pulled, galleys are carried to a long rectangular steel table, called the collating bank. There, if time permits, the type is assembled in proper sequence—as indicated by the identification slug affixed to each take—and distributed to the page form. But if the clock is pushing deadline, the galleys are rushed to the stone with the takes still out of sequence, and the printer making up the page assembles the type as he places it in the chase. Corrections, too, are piling up beside the printer, but only if they're marked "Must" does he attempt to make them now. The others will be dropped in between editions.

Make-up editors bend over the forms as the printers deftly fit the pieces into place. If a story doesn't fit, the editor bites it off at the end or removes a nonessential paragraph in the middle. If copy is missing, he sets up a search; if a head doesn't fit, he calls the copydesk that wrote it and asks that they try again.

Occasionally, it works the other way, and a copydesk asks the make-up editor to alter a page layout to permit a different type headline. Tonight, Jack Badiner, the foreign desk slot man, calls David Lidman in the composing room. Would it be possible, Badiner asks, to provide more space for the jump head on the story about the Dutch bishops permitting married priests to preach? The story, Badiner explains, is complicated. It begins at the bottom of page 1 with a head that reads: "Dutch Approve Role/For Married Priests." It jumps into page 10, where the layout calls for another single-column head that does not permit even that many words.

"Can we have a 'Ribbon Six' instead?" Badiner asks, referring to a single line across six columns. This would give the headline writer more space to clarify an intricate and delicate subject. Lidman checks the page 10 layout. He can switch it around. The Ribbon Six comes up the pneumatic tube. It says: "Dutch Bishops Agree to Let Married Priests Preach in Experimental Rite."

Pages are closing now at the rate of three every five minutes, as they must. The women's page has gone; the flags are up on the financial pages. At 8:25, Bob Barzilay, make-up editor on the editorial page, signals the printer, "Let it go." Right on the nose, though it had looked for a few hectic moments as if the page would be late. There had been a last-minute remake.

                                                              • • •

At 8:10, as A. H. Raskin finished his last chore of the day—editing week-end editorials—he had a call from Harvey Segal, the board's economics specialist who had written the editorial on the Nixon Administration's bank regulation bill.

"I've been talking to friends in Washington," Segal told him, "and they indicate the shape of the bill is still indefinite. I think we ought to hold the editorial out pending further verification."

Raskin leafed quickly through the proofs of editorials in type. He selected one, approximately the same length as the bank piece, that urged a swift start on a fourth jetport for the

New York area. He called Barzilay in the composing room and told him to make the substitution.

Barzilay and the printer working with him glance at the clock. Not much time. First, locate the "jetport" type. It's a little shorter than the Segal piece it replaces; the lines must be spaced out. This process—adjusting type to fit the space perfectly so that the page will lock up securely—is known as justifying the page. The printer's fingers move skillfully over the inky surface, inserting leads, thin metal strips that will increase the space between the lines of type. The page gets away on time.

· · ·

At 8:35, Lewis Jordan and Larry Hauck go to the composing room to close the edition. They leave Tom Daffron on watch in the bullpen. He will notify them if anything unforeseen occurs between now and 9:15, when the edition closes. Daffron came in half an hour ago and has been reading the summaries and studying page layouts, familiarizing himself with the news and how it is being presented. He'll keep the late watch in the bullpen and steer the paper through the late editions.

As Jordan and Hauck step onto the composing-room floor from the tiny elevator that runs between the third and fourth floors, their eyes rest on the page-closing scoreboard under the clock. Twenty-eight pages have been locked up and wheeled away to the stereotypers. Thirty-six to go—in forty minutes. Okay.

They turn their attention to page 1, which is beginning to fill with type under the swift-moving fingers of Frank Gilroy, a husky hunk of man in a short-sleeved T shirt over which he wears the printer's traditional ink-stained apron. "No problems," Gilroy assures the editors, without breaking stride. Fingers in constant motion, beads of perspiration on his brow, he lifts type and headlines from galleys lined up on the stone and places them in the page form in the position indicated on the page layout beside him.

Jordan and Hauck step a few feet to the editors' desk to read proofs of page 1 stories. As they spot errors, they mark them and send them back to the machines as a double check in case the proofroom missed them. If a sentence seems awkward or unclear, they rephrase it. They check proofs of page 1 headlines. If they think alterations are called for, they ask the news desk for a revision or, if time is short, rewrite it themselves. Page 1, the showcase page, must go in, even in the first edition, as clean as it is humanly possible to make it.

• • •

8:55. Forty-three pages gone. Twenty-one to go in twenty minutes. The pace must quicken. One page a minute is the quota now. Unless it is maintained, pages will pile up in the stereotype department and delay the press run.

Nancy Moran, the leggy young brunette who prepares the "News Summary and Index" at the bottom of the split page, is at a desk in the corner of the composing room refining the copy she sent up earlier, checking page references to make sure stories have been placed in the pages indicated on the dummies. It's possible, in the last-minute rush of getting an edition to press, that an expected advertisement doesn't materialize or that a story comes out longer, or shorter, than anticipated, and the make-up editors sometimes have to shift layouts quickly. Tonight, for example, a column of sports news has slopped over onto a financial page. It will be pulled back between editions, but meanwhile it must be correctly indexed. Joe Prisco, the make-up editor on the sports pages, informs Miss Moran. She makes the change: "Lipton Cup yacht race starts today off Miami, P. 40." All other sports stories are on pages 36 through 39.

Miss Moran's newsroom desk has been awash all evening with story summaries and page dummies. From this mass of paper she has selected the big news—the page 1 stories and related inside stories—and has written forty- to sixty-word capsule summaries of each to run under "The Major Events of the Day." Every other story longer than 200 words she has listed under "The Other News."

As her copy comes off the linotype, a printer working next to the machine places it in a six-column box which will be dropped, as a unit, at the last minute, in the page form. She is cutting back here, expanding there, checking page references. The box must be precise in length and accurate in page references.

The forms still open are filling swiftly now. Heads join up with type, maps and pictures slide into the exact positions left for them. Proofroom corrections pour from the machines. If there's time, they will be placed in the forms. If not, they will be held until the next edition. Pages cannot be held up now without throwing the whole production of the paper out of gear.

• • •

The rat-a-tat of printers' mallets fills the great chamber, the signal that pages are closing with speed and precision. There are still holes in the middle of Semple's story from Paris, awaiting the garbled takes that had to be resent. At 8:55, a fresh insert from Semple drops on the copy cutters' desk. The foreign desk instructs Lidman where to make room for it in the story.

Semple had hung around the Hotel Georges Cinq waiting for the "pool report" from the small group of reporters who had attended the formal dinner at the Elysée Palace. It was past midnight when they arrived to fill in the waiting reporters. What they had to say suggested that Nixon had revived some of his effusive language from his prepared airport remarks and inserted it into his formal toast. It is worth an insert, Semple thinks, if only to strengthen the point that Nixon is going all-out in Paris to melt the ice with de Gaulle and enlist him in a variety of common causes.

He sits down at a typewriter and bangs out a paragraph: "Some of the praise in Mr. Nixon's unused text did, in fact, creep into his toast tonight at a formal dinner at the Elysée Palace when he described the General's career as an 'epic of courage' and cited his 'wisdom and vision—the vision that sees beyond the crisis of the moment, that sees the great forces that are at play in the world.' "

He files it to New York with instructions to the desk as to where it should be inserted in his story.

The day's events are swirling in his mind as he rides the hotel elevator to the suite he is sharing with Max Frankel. It occurs to him that he, in Paris, and the first edition in New York are going to bed at about the same time.

The Presses Roll

· · · · · · · · · · · · **9 p.m.**

Fifteen minutes to deadline. Fifteen pages still open. The rhythm is right. A page a minute.

A galley of type is rushed to the page 9 chase. Bernard Weinraub has updated his story on the *Pueblo* hearing in Coronado. The hearing ended early today, 4:30 California time. No fireworks at the afternoon session. The story he filed during the noon recess holds up. But an insert had to be made to indicate that it covers the whole day's proceedings. He flipped through a carbon of the copy he had already filed. One paragraph would do it. He typed it out, sent it to New York by Western Union with the message: "Please insert after paragraph 4, take 5 ending 'mopping his forehead with a handkerchief.'"

Sometimes, when the hearing drags on late or when the afternoon session yields the essence of the day's news, Weinraub can't make the first edition and the national desk has to use agency copy. But today he has overcome the three-hour time difference. "You're clear," Chick Butsikares tells him when he calls the desk to make sure everything is okay. "You made it."

Time is precious now. Decisions are made quickly. Editors move with assurance: Let's make this correction; let's wait on that one; let's get this page away. They know that less damage will be done by a bad decision that can be corrected in the next edition than by a slow one that will disrupt the production schedule.

9:10. Four pages to go—in five minutes.

The big block of type that is the "News Summary and Index" is placed in the hole awaiting it at the bottom of the split page. Nancy Moran makes a final check of page references. If there are errors now, she will have to wait until the next edition to correct them. The printer justifies the type, locks up the page. At 9:11, the flag goes up.

Page 36, the first "Sports" page, is still open. The half-time score at the Princeton-Columbia basketball game comes from the linotype. One sentence: "Princeton took a 33–32 lead at halftime." It is inserted high up in Gordon White's story on the game, written in advance. He will rewrite in full for later editions.

Page 3 is under the printer's mallet. Bob Semple's insert on the Nixon-de Gaulle dinner is in place.

A head is missing from page 1. At 9:14 it is slapped down on the stone. Printer Frank Gilroy fits it neatly into its exact space, the final piece in the jigsaw puzzle. Jordan bends over to read it. "Okay," he tells Gilroy. "Let it go." Gilroy tightens the quoins that lock the type firmly in the chase, and planes the page with mallet and hammer. At 9:15, to the split second, it is wheeled away on the first leg of its journey to the presses.

• • •

The composing-room phase of getting out the edition is ended —on time. Tension slackens. An eerie silence fills the great chamber which seconds earlier reverberated to a cacophony of rat-a-tats. Printers doff their aprons and go across the street for a beer or upstairs to the cafeteria for a sandwich. The editors return to the newsroom, now almost deserted, the desks manned by skeleton crews. It's the between-editions supper break.

The action is concentrated now in the cavernous, two-story

basement pressroom where 106 press units, each weighing twenty-five tons, are immovably set in bedrock 34 feet below the pavement. Their gigantic metal frames—some black, some blue, some fireman's red—seem to lock together. Each unit prints sixteen pages and is linked by a web of newsprint to neighboring units to form a press. The metal monsters consume more than 370,000 tons of newsprint and 6,000 tons of ink each year. Unrolled, the newsprint would create a carpet of paper nearly 3 million miles long—more than five round trips to the moon.

Twelve presses have been made ready to print tonight's sixty-four-page paper, each consisting of four units. (Others will be running off advance sections of Sunday's paper.) Each of the twelve will spew out 40,000 papers an hour, completely printed, folded and counted. Each is manned by a pressman-in-charge and a crew of twelve journeymen with printer's ink on their arms and shirts and the pressman's trademark on their heads—little square paper caps to protect their hair against grease and ink spray.

Pressmen are more a part of their machinery than are any other workers in a newspaper plant. They study the massive, intricate mechanism. They move, with sure step, to fill the huge oil wells that grease all moving parts, to check the ink fountains fed from ink storage tanks.

Now they are threading up and plating up. They thread the newsprint into position, feeding it through the presses from giant newsprint rolls in the reel room, one floor below. Automatic "flying pasters" splice spent rolls to fresh so that once a press starts to roll, the sheets move through in continuous stream.

Mechanical conveyor belts crawl, wormlike, along the concrete floor, alive with curved metal plates issuing from the adjoining stereotype department. There are twelve plates of each page, one for each press, and on each plate the page number is inked in bold black figures. Plate boys, stationed at each unit, are on the alert for specific page numbers. As the plates march past, like a parade of big silver-backed turtles, the boys pick them off the conveyor, stack them by the unit and note the arrival time on a blackboard. Pressmen lock them in position on the press cylinder.

At 9:30, the "starter" plates emerge from the stereo-casting pots and rumble along the conveyor belt. Plate boys pluck them off and post the final page number on their scoreboards. The "starter" is the last page closed in the composing room, the last page cast into metal, the last page locked on the press. When it is in place, the press-start signal is given.

At 9:32, seventeen minutes after the last page closed in the composing room, the starter button is pressed.

The great machines wind up slowly. The crews watch, hawk-eyed, making sure that sheets are feeding into folders, that ink feeds are working, that all pages are in proper position. Then the "let go" button is pressed. Faster and faster move the webs of paper until the air is filled with such a thunderous roar that a man can speak to his neighbor only by shouting close to his ear.

Streams of printed and folded papers pour from the maws of the metal monsters—ten papers every second from each press. They climb in continuous line through spring-wire escalators to the mail room, one floor above, at street level. There they are automatically stacked, tied into bundles and whisked by conveyor into waiting delivery trucks backed up at loading platforms.

• • •

Because news is perishable, newspaper distribution is a high-speed, ulcer-breeding vocation. Most manufacturers can allow themselves some time margin for delivery. But the almost-one-million copies of The Times that will be printed tonight must be on their way to readers the moment they leap from the presses. If the paper is not in its regular spot at the regular time, no excuse satisfies the customers.

The Times's distribution problem is more complex than most because it is a national and international, as well as local, newspaper, and because it has some 35,000 subscribers who are served individually by mail. While the bulk of the circulation is concentrated in New York City and the area called suburban—within fifty miles of the city—240,000 copies of tonight's paper will fan out to more than 11,000 cities and towns between the coasts, to foreign countries and to United States possessions.

Most of the papers now roaring from the presses are headed for distant points—28,500 to Boston; 13,000 to Miami; 2,600 to Los Angeles; 138 to Multnomah County, Oregon; 9 to Amarillo, Texas. Circulation men, as familiar with plane and train schedules as are airline and railroad information bureaus, have booked their passage, and loaded trucks now carry them to terminals to start them on their journey.

When enough papers have been printed to meet these "must" circulation schedules, the presses, on a signal from the mailroom, will be halted to await the next edition.

That one—the first Late City—will close at midnight, two and a quarter hours from now, and there is much to be done in the meantime.

The editors turn their attention first to the edition coming off the presses. At 9:41, a copyboy brings the first copies to the newsroom and distributes them to all desks.

The bullpen editors, joined by Make-up Editor David Lidman and the night picture editor, go at once into a post-mortem conference. They flip through the paper, page by page, suggesting typographical or picture changes that will enhance its appearance, correcting nuances, checking headlines to make sure they tell the story properly.

"The head on Finney's story goes too far," Ted Bernstein says, referring to John Finney's piece, slugged "Intelsat," about Russia's position in the communications satellite negotiations. The head says: "Soviet Backs Single Satellite Network." Tom Daffron, who will take charge in the bullpen when the other editors leave, makes a note. (In later editions the head was altered to "Soviet Hints It Backs a Single Satellite Network.")

"This head on Eboli," Bernstein says, pointing to a one-paragraph story on page 18. "If he had a heart attack, as the *Daily News* says, our head should say so." Thomas Eboli, a reputed top underworld figure, had collapsed on the witness stand during a rackets investigation hearing the day before and had been rushed to the hospital. The *Daily News* played it big tonight, but The Times has only a two-inch paragraph with a small, one-line K-head that says: "Eboli Resting Comfortably."

Daffron jots down a reminder to have a rewrite man check it out.

"We've got twenty columns of overset," Lidman reports—twenty columns that did not get into the edition because there was no space. Between now and the next edition, space must be made for it as well as for copy scheduled to come in later, such as critics' reviews and new stories pegged to events taking place during the evening.

How did the news happen to run twenty columns over its 205-column estimate? Partly because of late-breaking developments, partly because stories scheduled for a certain length reached the copydesk hard on deadline and were sent to the composing room in takes, a paragraph or two at a time, making it difficult for the copyreader to trim it to size in time for the first edition.

Advertising is over, too. Ray Nelan sticks his head into the bullpen conference. "We're three columns over on ads," he reports. Instead of 307 columns of ads, there are 310 in the edition. How come? Advertising make-up men, gambling that there wouldn't be too much overset news, had put through a few extra ads that came in after the estimate had been made up.

So advertising is occupying three columns that news is entitled to. It's up to the bullpen to decide if it needs all its space or if it can make do with less. The editors run through the twenty galleys of overset to see how much is essential copy that must be fitted into the next edition. They check the list of stories to come and stories in the pipeline—still being set in the composing room and not yet in proof. The list is long.

"Kill those three columns, Ray," Bernstein orders.

· · · · · · · · · · · · 10 p.m.

It's kill or cut now. Seventeen columns must come out of the first edition to provide space for the overset and for late news.

The supper break is ended, and shirt-sleeved copyreaders take their places again around the rims of the horseshoe-shaped desks. Each man turns first to the stories he processed; he patches up imprecise phrases, rewrites awkward headlines, checks them for length and for typographical errors and sends corrections to the composing room. There are a few empty chairs now around the rims. The stagger system under which the desks operate provides for full strength during the peak early evening hours leading up to the first edition, and shorter staffs when the copy load is lighter.

On each of the main news desks—foreign, national and metropolitan—clerks go swiftly through the paper and mark with red crayon every story that falls within its quota. Then they go through the overset galleys, crayoning the copy that has been squeezed out: some whole stories and some bites or tail ends that couldn't be fitted into the page form. They add up the crayoned lines with ten-column tape measures and, from the desk editor at their side, get an estimate of how much space will be required for new stories in the next edition. They scribble their findings on the Space Report—

"allotted," "overset," "in 1st edition," "2nd edition needs"—
and hurry the figures to the bullpen.

Lewis Jordan scans the Space Reports when the bullpen
conference breaks up a few minutes after 10. Having determined each desk's quota in midafternoon, in midevening he
must hold them to it. He issues cut orders.

"Cut five columns," he tells Allan Siegal, who has taken
over as night editor on the foreign desk.

Siegal instructs his copyreaders to accommodate the bites in
the overset by trimming material out of the body of the bitten
stories. Or if, in their judgment, a story stands up as is, to kill
the bites.

The four final paragraphs in David Binder's story on the
Berlin crisis, which leads the paper, have ended up in the
overset and Siegal wants them in the paper; they add an important element to the story. He goes through the piece carefully, trying to find something else to eliminate instead.
But it's tightly written, and important; it's got to run in full.
He confers with David Lidman. Between them they arrange
to move the jump on "Berlin" into a larger hole on a different page. "But you'll have to make a few trims elsewhere,"
Lidman tells him.

The make-up editors get similar requests from other editors
sweating out the paring process. "I've got three new spreads,"
George Barrett, now in charge on the metropolitan desk, tells
them. "What can you do for me?"

It's a game of accommodation. Trim this picture, or drop
it. Kill that short. Cut that spread. The wordy story goes
down. The nonessential goes out. The story that looked important at 7 o'clock isn't so important at 10 o'clock. Knock it
down.

Or, occasionally, build one up.

The Nixon jump, with pictures, fills nearly the whole of
page 3. Siegal, whose shape attests to the fact that he's a gour-
mand, if not a gourmet, notes a gap in the tale. What was the

menu at the dinner de Gaulle served Nixon? He recalls reading in raw copy a short sent from Paris by John Hess, listing
the menu, plus wines. The dayside cast it aside, but Siegal figures it would make a nice box and dress up the appearance of
the page. He digs it out and deals it to Oliver Howard, a
copyreader who spends his vacations sampling the lush restaurants of France, a man Siegal knows will treat it with
love. From Howard's end of the desk comes lip-smacking,
then a guffaw.

Hess, a food lover who formerly worked out of the home
office, has remembered the saloon across the street where 43d
Street deskmen spend their inelegant supper hours. After cata-
loguing the Elysée foie gras and Bordeaux, he signed off his
copy: FINIS. TO GOUGH'S.

. . .

There's a difference of opinion among the foreign deskmen as
to the correct pronunciation of Les Halles, the Paris market
featured on tonight's split page. The story includes the pho-
netic spelling. Siegal shoots off a cable to Jim Brown in the
Paris bureau: MY MEMORY, UNDER ATTACK BY
SKEPTICS, SUDDENLY GROWS UNCERTAIN. IS LES
HALLES PRONOUNCED LAY AHL OR LAY ZAHL?
THANKS AND REGARDS.

The answer comes back: PRONOUNCE IT LAY AHL. IT
IS AN EXCEPTION TO THE RULE.

. . .

The bullpen, turning its attention to the next edition, asks Sie-
gal where the Syrian story stands. Siegal had gotten a cable
from Jim Brown a few minutes before 10, saying: SPOKE TO
SCHMIDT ON THE PHONE. HE SAID HE WOULD
PHONE BACK TO PARIS AS SOON AS POSSIBLE WITH
ANSWERS.

Now it is well past 10 o'clock and nothing further has been
heard from Brown or from Schmidt. The editors know that
instant communications from Beirut can, at times, be far from

instant. What are the alternatives? United Press International, which sent the first bulletin on Syria more than two hours ago, has fleshed out its story with some details and background. As has Reuters, which is now sending a story that speaks not of a coup but of a shift in power.

They decide to use the Reuters story if Schmidt doesn't come through in time for the edition that closes at midnight. They will place it at the bottom of page 1 under a small one-column head, a substitute for the first-edition story in that spot about Switzerland's protest to the Arab world over the attack on an Israeli jet. The Swiss story will go inside.

Siegal informs David Lidman that "Syria" will run about 750 words. He's not guessing that that is what the story, when it is all in, will come to. He's judging what it is worth in comparison with the rest of the foreign report.

• • •

Across the room, the six men on the rewrite battery are posted like sentinels in the front line of reporters' desks. Behind them stretches a sea of emptiness. They are the only reporters on the floor. If crisis explodes anywhere from now on through the night, they will hold the line and produce whatever is called for. They will also produce the less explosive copy— the inserts fitted without seams; the background, literal and substantial. They are the firemen on guard. By telephone, by research, they do the flash work.

Siegal stops by Robert McFadden's desk, which is buried under morgue folders marked "Syria."

"I hate these goddamn attempts at instant expertise," McFadden, nose-deep in the politics of the Baath party, mutters. Siegal offers mild sympathy, tells him that his background piece will run as a follow to the Reuters story and asks him to hold it to half a column if possible.

• • •

At an adjoining desk, Larry Van Gelder is checking the *Daily News* story that says Thomas Eboli suffered a heart attack when he collapsed at a rackets hearing yesterday. The *Daily News* attributes the statement to officials at University Hospital, where Eboli is a patient. Van Gelder has the hospital on the phone and is getting the usual bureaucratic runaround. He insists that he talk to someone in authority. He finally gets to the nurse in charge of the hospital at night. She doesn't know where the *Daily News* got its information. Besides, she says, the hospital never reveals diagnoses. Mr. Eboli is resting comfortably, she says, and that is precisely what the headline on page 18 says.

Van Gelder passes this information to George Barrett, who relays it to Tom Daffron, from whom the request for a check on Eboli's condition came in the first place. As Van Gelder returns to his desk, he muses that much of rewrite consists of checking out stories in the *Daily News*.

Barrett asks him to take a couple of inserts from Robert Smith in Plainfield, New Jersey. "And tell him to keep them short. Like one sentence." Van Gelder laughs.

Smith had gone to Plainfield at 6 o'clock to relieve Barnard Collier, who returned to the office to write about the black-white confrontation sparked by trouble in the city's schools. Now Smith is on the phone to report what has occurred during the evening. He has assembled his notes, pages of them, and is ready to dictate. Van Gelder warns him to keep it short. Smith moans, reorganizes his material, mentally slices it down, and dictates a few sentences. Van Gelder takes them on the typewriter.

"You wouldn't believe how much work I did to get those inserts," Smith groans. "I've been working steadily since I got here."

• • •

Al Blayer and Ray Cooper from the production department stop by the bullpen to find out exactly how the editors plan to play the "Ike" story. They've got to know if there is to be any deviation from normal routine that will affect the mechanics of getting late editions printed and distributed.

Bernstein runs through the plans: the full four-page obituary will go in if Eisenhower dies before midnight; if he dies after midnight, the abbreviated piece will be used with a note explaining that the detailed obituary will appear the following day.

"We've got a deathwatch," Bernstein tells the production men. "We're staying open until 3:45 A.M."

They hurry off the floor to juggle their schedules. Printers must be held overtime in the composing room. Press runs and delivery routines must be altered. They will hold back on the final press run so that if Eisenhower dies between 3 A.M., the normal closing time, and 3:45, the story will get into a substantial number of papers. It would make no sense to print papers and never have them get out of the plant.

There are four regularly scheduled editions a night: the first, or City, now on the presses (which is, in effect, a misnomer, for its distribution, except to some city newsstands, is national), two Late City editions and a Cleanup edition. The City and the two Late Cities can be postscripted—the press run interrupted, that is—if a story develops that is important enough to get on the street immediately. Should Eisenhower die tonight, whatever edition is on the press at the hour of death will be postscripted. The Cleanup edition is actually a postscript to the Late City final. It goes to press at the final moment before the newsroom shuts down for the night. It is The End. It includes stories of consequence that break after the Late City final, and all possible corrections of errors. It is the cleanest of the night, the edition that goes into the files, to libraries and on to microfilm. It is today's *New York Times* honed, as nearly as possible, to perfection.

By 10:30 P.M., the men in the bullpen who have steered the first edition to completion, patched it up and prettied it up and mapped plans for subsequent editions, are ready to leave. Tom Daffron, whose gray-haired cherubic appearance belies his news savvy, will carry through. If anything of major importance develops, he will get in touch with the top editors at their homes.

Copy is flowing again from the copydesks up the pneumatic tube to the composing room—some of it new, some of it corrections, some of it trims. The make-up editors, with their revised page dummies, have returned to the composing room to direct the closing of pages for the next edition. Printers bend again over the page forms, inserting new type as it comes from the linotypes. Every one of the sixty-four pages has been opened up—some for minor corrections, some for major revisions.

· · ·

In the New Orleans courtroom where the Clay Shaw trial is in evening session, Martin Waldron glances at his watch. 9:40. 10:40 in New York. He'd better get to a phone and telephone a new lead for the next edition.

He dials the 43d Street recording room. "New lead from Waldron," he tells the recording-room operator and begins to dictate from notes: "The chief defense attorney for Clay L. Shaw charged in his closing argument to the jury tonight that District Attorney Jim Garrison had brought Mr. Shaw to trial only to give himself a forum in which to attack the Warren Commission."

He goes on for 250 words. "That's all. Okay?" he asks. The operator has monitored the dictation and has no questions. Before he hangs up, Waldron asks him to inform the national desk that the court is still in session and that the judge hopes the case will go to the jury tonight. He'll be back with more later.

The new lead is on the national desk by 10:50. It is read and ordered as a top to the first-edition story, which is trimmed of less essential elements to make room for it. It is in type before the composing room faces the last-minute spurt of copy from critics, sports writers and other staffers on night assignments.

The cultural news pages have gaping holes. Carry-over reviews, slated only for the first edition, have been removed from the forms to await new appraisals from critics who have hurried back to the office from performances all over the city. They are at their typewriters, under deadline pressure. Copyboys stand by to rush their reviews, take by take, to the copydesk for processing.

· · · · · · · · · · · **11 p.m.**

It's noon in Saigon. Terry Smith and Charlie Mohr are in the bureau, reading the fronting cable that has just arrived from New York. It tells them how the first edition shapes up. The fronting is sent by the foreign news desk to all its correspondents, wherever they may be, immediately after the first edition is up. It gives them the total world picture and, just as important, informs them of the fate of their own stories.

The lengthy cable summarizes all stories on page 1 and all inside foreign stories, and lists those that have been held over, killed or shorted—ended up as four paragraphs or less. Each summary includes the story's place of origin and the writer's name.

Smith and Mohr read it with interest.

UNICOL * LEAD BERLIN (BINDER) SOVIET THREATENS CURB ON TRAFFIC ON BERLIN ROUTES, OFFLEAD'S PARIS (SEMPLE) NIXON CALLS FOR AN END TO "OLD QUARRELS."

ALSO FRONTED: SAIGON (SMITH) G.I.'S BATTLE FOE ON EDGE OF SAIGON IN DAY-LONG CLASH, PRAGUE (RANDAL) PRAGUE REJECTS A DICTATED UNITY, GENEVA (HAMILTON) SWISS SEND PROTEST TO THREE ARAB NATIONS, THE HAGUE

* One-column.

(SPECIAL) * DUTCH APPROVE ROLE FOR MARRIED PRIESTS, LOS ANGELES (ROBINSON) SIRHAN PLEA TO DIE IS DENIED BY COURT, WASHINGTON (BEL-AIR) EISENHOWER IS "WEAKER" AS PNEUMONIA DEVELOPS, WASHINGTON (BLAIR) HICKEL OUT-LINES POLLUTION CURBS, WASHINGTON (WELLES) U.S. VOICES CONCERN ON BERLIN TO SOVIET, LOCAL (KING) AGENCY SHOP WON BY MUNICIPAL UNIONS, LOCAL (KOSHETZ) THEFTS REDUCED IN GARMENT AREA, LOCAL (KIHSS) SOME GAINS FOUND FOR URBAN NEGROES.

INSIDED: ROME (DOTY) PRESIDENT AND ITAL-IAN LEADERS FIND WIDE AGREEMENT IN TALKS, BRUSSELS (MIDDLETON) NATO PREPARING A RE-PORT ON WHEN, HOW AND WHERE TO USE NUCLEAR ARMS, MOSCOW (KAMM) ENVOYS IN SOVIET GLOOMIER, BUCHAREST (SZULC) CEAUSESCU SEEKS SUPPORT, MADRID (EDER) LEAK IN U.S. ON BASE TALKS IRKS SPAIN, TOKYO (OKA) ON A HILL IN TOKYO A HAVEN OF PEACE BECOMES A FOCUS OF DISCORD, PARIS (HOFMANN) NIXON TO CON-FER WITH KY IN PARIS, DAUTIENG (MOHR) U.S. POST USES "KILLER JUNIOR" WHEN MASSED ENEMY ATTACKS, JERUSALEM (FERON) ESHKOL BURIED, PARIS (HESS) THE FOOD BASKET OF PARIS TRANS-FERS TO THE SUBURBS, LONDON (LEE) ELIZABETH TWO WORK SATISFIES EXPERT.

SHORTED: HONGKONG (DURDIN) SATO, LONDON (EMERSON) SABBATH, LISBON (HOWES) DEMON-STRATION.

HELDOVER: LONDON (SHUSTER) GAMBLE, MOS-COW (GWERTZMAN) TEAPOT, NAIROBI (FELLOWS) RAIN.

* The story carried no byline, just an agate "Special to the New York Times" credit line.

Smith and Mohr now know how their stories are played—
Smith on page 1, Mohr inside.

. . .

Daylight, thin and purple, is creeping through the windows of
the London bureau as the fronting cable chatters in shortly
after 6 A.M. Ralph Berry, the overnight wire-room operator, is
the lone man on duty. He reads it over a cup of tea brewed
for him by the cleaning ladies who are tidying up the offices,
then relays it to Tad Szulc in Bucharest, David Binder in Berlin, Jonathan Randal in Prague and James Feron in Jerusalem.

In Africa, the Far East, South America, Australia—
wherever in the world a Times man is on duty—the fronting
is greeted like a letter from home. No matter how remote a
correspondent's post, he knows how today's paper shapes up
before most readers in New York City have seen it, before the
Late City edition goes to press.

That edition is closing now.

. . .

At 11:19, the green "stop-the-press" light flashes, the signal
that enough copies of the City edition have been run off to
meet the circulation department's plane, train and truck
schedules. The plates are removed from the cylinders, piled on
trucks and wheeled away to the stereotype shop to be dumped
into the melting pot. Newly molded plates for the next edition
crawl along the conveyor toward the presses.

By 11:30, the critics' reviews have cleared the copydesk.
They were written hurriedly, processed swiftly. There will be
time after the midnight edition closes to tidy them up for the
Late City final. Four music reviews tonight and Clive Barnes's
appraisal of the Joffrey Ballet at City Center.

Barnes, who is lightning fast on a typewriter, batted out his
600-word review in thirty-five minutes, then followed it to the
composing room to make corrections in proof. By 11:40 he is
clear—and on the way to his next assignment. This one is at

Fillmore East, a pop palace in Manhattan's East Village, this year's "now" place. The show there goes on at midnight, and he wants to view it as a theatrical happening, possible fodder for a future review. The Joshua Light Show and two British groups—Ten Years After and John Mayall—are the come-on.

• • •

Before Tom Daffron goes to the composing room to close the edition, he confers with Arthur Reed, the national desk slot man who, at this hour, is the editor in charge on his desk. Reed has just talked with David Rosenbaum, the night man in the Washington bureau. Rosenbaum has told him there will be no more bulletins on Ike tonight.

"If he dies it will be on the wires immediately," Reed reports to Daffron, "and we will call Felix Belair at his home to update the lead, if necessary. I've given the bureau good night."

It's 11:45—zero hour for inserting the full four-page obituary. If Eisenhower dies between now and 3:45 A.M., it will be the abbreviated obit. Daffron instructs Reed to prepare two headlines against that eventuality—an R-head (two lines across two columns) for page 1, and a binder (one line across the top of the page) for the jump.

The scene in the composing room shortly before midnight is a replay of three hours earlier. Once again the clock's hands race toward deadline, and the staccato rat-a-tat of printers' mallets indicates that pages are closing swiftly. By 11:30, fifty-five of the sixty-four pages have gone. By 11:55, the scoreboard under the clock shows three to go—pages 1, 11 and 36.

A hole at the bottom of page 1 is being fitted with the Syrian story. It jumps into page 11. Ted Levene, a foreign desk copyreader—who, in spite of his name, is the resident expert on Arabs—has welded the Reuters and McFadden stories into a coherent whole. Siegal decided definitely to go with Reuters in this edition after Jim Brown informed him by cable from Paris at 11:10: HAVE BOOKED FURTHER CALL TO BEIRUT BUT AS YET HAVEN'T HEARD FROM SCHMIDT. STANDING BY.

Levene sent the last take of the agency story and the headline—"A Shift in Power/In Syria Is Reported"—to the composing room at 11:40. Now it is being placed in the page form. The flag goes up on page 11 at 11:56, on page 1 at 11:57.

Page 36, a sports page, is the starter, the last page to close. It has been torn apart between editions, and space-holders have been removed to make room for live copy—stories, pictures and scores of night basketball games. The page is now dominated by a spectacular, down-from-the-basket picture of a blocked shot taken by Mike Lien at the Columbia-Princeton game.

When the game ended at 9:20, Lien caught a subway back to the 43d Street lab, hoping he had something dramatic. He had shot from an unusual angle—the running track that circles the Columbia gym above court level. He whistled with pleasure as his negatives emerged from the lab's high-speed processing machine. Joe Prisco, the sports page make-up editor, was so struck with the picture that he rearranged his page still further to give it booming display. It's in the form now, a deep four-column cut under a binder head proclaiming Princeton the Ivy League champions and alongside Gordon White's story of the game, sent by Western Union from the press box in the gym.

At 11:59, Prisco tells the printer to let the page go. The second edition is on its way—one minute ahead of schedule.

. . .

The lights in the Paris bureau are still ablaze as dawn breaks over the city on the Seine. Jim Brown has finally gotten through to Schmidt in Beirut and has turned the phone over to Denis Powel, the bureau's late deskman, who returned to the office when he learned about the coup in Syria. Powel is at the typewriter, headset on, taking Schmidt's dictation.

"I guess that wraps it up," Schmidt tells him after he has dictated 500 words. At either end of the line the two men, with a single thought, glance at their watches. Schmidt's points to 7 o'clock. It's an hour earlier in Paris. It's midnight in New York.

Edition times are engraved on their minds. Too late, they know, for the first Late City.

"We'll make the final," Powel assures him.

· · · · · · · · · · · midnight

The fastest, surest and most efficient way to get the story to New York, Powel knows, is by telephone. No chance of transmission garbles and time-consuming delays in straightening them out.

He reaches for the telephone and asks the overseas operator for an unlisted number in New York. One ring, and the recording-room operator on 43d Street is on the line.

"This is Denis Powel in Paris. I have a piece here from Dana Schmidt in Beirut."

The operator turns on the recorder attached to the telephone. "Okay," he tells Powel, "you can start."

It takes Powel six minutes to dictate. It takes the operator another eleven minutes to transcribe. He sends it out to the foreign desk, take by take.

Siegal is amazed when, unannounced, the story begins to stream from the recording room. It's the first he knows that Paris has made contact with Schmidt. It all happened so quickly—from Beirut to Paris to New York in less than half an hour—that there was no time or reason to send an advisory that it was on the way.

As he begins to read Schmidt's story, Siegal is struck with the fact that here is a classic example of why The Times maintains its own correspondents rather than rely on wire

1 a.m.

The newsroom is on dogwatch, a desert with a small oasis of editors, deskmen, rewrite men, clerks and copyboys. The late man on each of the main news desks is alone now; the rims are empty.

Thirty-five of the sixty-four pages for the Late City final edition are open in the composing room. Corrections and new copy are moving toward them. Minor trims by each desk will take care of the small amount of overset left out of the second edition. Within the hour the pages will begin their third journey of the night through the mat-making and plate-casting machines and on to the press cylinders.

Shortly after 1 A.M., Seymour Topping calls Siegal from his home in Scarsdale. Topping likes to check in around bedtime. There are some questions on which he alone can act, such as giving a correspondent permission to make a proposed trip away from home base. He wants to know, too, in these middle-of-the-night calls, about any newly arrived messages. If they are urgent, he dictates answers.

Tonight there are no messages requiring his attention. Siegal tells him what happened in Syria and how it is being handled.

Topping wonders if there is any point in sending Schmidt to Syria, and decides there is not. With censorship and primitive filing facilities, a correspondent would find himself largely helpless there. Better to stay at the central listening post, Beirut, and rely on diplomats and intelligence men. Besides, there are the tensions of Arab-Israeli relations to monitor, another job best done in Beirut.

At 1:15, the Associated Press wire carries a story about trouble at Cornell. Daffron confers with Dick Roberts. They decide to put it on page 28, as a top to an earlier agency story about riots at a Michigan college. Roberts tells Bill Chambers, alone now on the make-up desk, that the new story is coming and instructs him to kill a few shorts on other nationwide school disturbances to make room for it.

At 1:21, Martin Waldron calls again from New Orleans. He dictates into a recorder a new 225-word lead: "Saturday, March 1—The Clay Shaw conspiracy trial went to the jury early today after District Attorney Jim Garrison of New Orleans said in a courtroom speech that 'powerful forces' in the United States were attempting to hide the truth about President Kennedy's death. . . ."

Daryl Frazell, on the national desk, cuts the new copy into Waldron's second-edition story and sends it to the composing room.

. . .

At 1:45, a Reuters bulletin shatters the newsroom quiet. It says: ARMED EAST GERMAN GUARDS HAVE ERECTED A ROADBLOCK ON THE MAIN AUTOBAHN LEADING TO WEST BERLIN.

This could be serious—the beginning of a major East-West confrontation. Daffron and Siegal go into a huddle. David Binder's story on the touchy situation, which leads the paper, talks about Soviet and East German threats to harass or cut transportation to Berlin. It also suggests that there might be temporary roadblocks because of Communist military maneuvers in the area. The Reuters bulletin is too brief to tell whether the new move is temporary or permanent.

Fifteen minutes to go before the Late City final closes. Daffron and Siegal must make a quick decision. Should they insert a brief, bracketed Reuters account of the roadblock high up in Binder's story?

But what if the roadblock is transitory or routine? There is the danger of fueling panic in a tense international situation. The importance of the East German move must be verified.

Siegal phones Reuters's New York bureau. "What is the rest of the story going to say?" he asks. The New York bureau doesn't know. The story has not yet been transmitted from London.

Daffron and Siegal decide not to rush into print with a vague indecisive fragment. The Late City final closes without reference to the roadblock.

They will recoup, if recoup they must, in a postscript.

· · · · · · · · · · · 2 a.m.

URGENT URGENT URGENT BINDER CAN YOU
GIVE US ANY DETAILS ON REUTERS REPORT THAT
EAST GERMANS CLOSED OFF AUTOBAHN WITH
METAL BARRIER AND ARMED MEN NEAR HELM-
STEDT? SIEGAL.

This triple-urgent query reaches the London bureau, for
relay to Binder, at 8 o'clock on a bright, crisp morning. John
Rothera, who has relieved Ralph Berry in the wire room, decides that the quickest way to get Binder is by telephone.

He reaches Binder in his hotel room in Berlin. While he's on
the phone, another message comes into London from Siegal:
LET ME KNOW WHERE IN BERLIN BINDER IS STAY-
ING AND HIS TELEPHONE NUMBER. WE ARE
TRYING TO REACH HIM BY PHONE FROM HERE.

Time is running out in New York, and Siegal is covering all
flanks. It might be faster to call Binder direct from 43d Street.

"They want your phone number in New York," Rothera
tells Binder.

Good idea, Binder thinks. It would be best to talk directly
to the office.

Rothera cables the number to Siegal.

Siegal gives it to Bob McFadden on rewrite. "Try your
damnedest to get through to him fast. The A.P. and U.P.I.

have corroborated the Reuters report on the roadblock. It sounds serious."

Fifty minutes to go before the Cleanup edition closes. Daffron prepares to build the one-column headline on Binder's story up to two columns unless Binder, when they reach him on the phone, feels strongly that this new development should not be played up. Siegal is set to edit a new lead from Binder or, if McFadden can't get through to him, to use one of the agency stories on the roadblock as a precede to the story now on the presses. No sweat. If they could just reach Binder.

• • •

At 2:12, Martin Waldron bolts from the courtroom of the Clay Shaw trial in New Orleans and calls Daryl Frazell on the national desk. "The verdict is in. Not guilty."

Frazell switches the call to Mark Hawthorne on rewrite. Waldron prepares to dictate the lead.

Daffron decides to postscript immediately. He wants to get the Shaw acquittal into as many papers as possible.

Frazell instructs Hawthorne to take a one-paragraph precede from Waldron. "Tell him we need it for the postscript. Then he can dictate a new lead for the final edition."

Waldron rattles off: "Clay L. Shaw was acquitted early today of a charge that he conspired to assassinate President Kennedy in 1963. The Criminal District Court Jury returned its verdict of not guilty after deliberating about fifty minutes."

A copyboy snatches it from Hawthorne's typewriter and runs it to Frazell. Frazell edits it swiftly and sends it to the composing room with a new head: "Shaw Acquitted / of 'Kennedy Plot.' "

• • •

There's an inexplicable delay on the overseas telephone circuit, and McFadden can't get through to Binder. Daffron decides to insert some mention of the roadblock in the postscript, anyhow, now that it has been confirmed by the other news services. Siegal edits one paragraph of the Reuters copy—"East Germany placed armed guards and a metal barrier Saturday morning at the entrance to the Berlin-bound Autobahn, halting all traffic, Reuters reports"—and orders it bracketed as an insert high up in Binder's story.

In the composing room, four pages are open to receive the postscript. The Shaw story is pulled from page 16 and placed on page 1, displacing the story on garment area thefts. That story has been trimmed to fit into its jump space on page 18. The split page with the "News Summary and Index" is open for revised page references to the "Shaw" and "Theft" stories.

At 2:39, the last of the postscripted pages are wheeled away to the stereo mat machines. They are on the presses at 2:45.

Meanwhile, Waldron has dictated to Hawthorne a 500-word new lead on the Shaw acquittal. Frazell has edited it, take by take, and sent it to the composing room to be set in type for the Cleanup edition.

• • •

At 2:40 in the morning, Bob McFadden finally gets through to David Binder in his hotel room in Berlin.

"Yes, I've heard of the Reuters report," Binder tells him, "and I've checked my sources here. I'm inclined to think the roadblock will be temporary. I think it's related to troop movements expected along the Autobahn. I don't think we should blow it up with a two-column head. I think we should just insert a mention of the roadblock in my story. I'll give you an insert."

He dictates: "This morning, East German troops blocked the main Berlin-bound Autobahn at Marienborn, its western entry point. They erected a metal barricade and stationed armed guards, stopping traffic. It appeared possible, however, that the measure was connected with forthcoming Soviet-block military maneuvers in the area and would only be temporary."

Daffron and Siegal are annoyed with Binder when they see what he has dictated. All three news agencies are providing vivid and somewhat spectacular eyewitness material on the erection of the roadblock. And there's Binder, in his hotel room, discounting the reports. A clear case, they agree, of a correspondent belittling a development because he personally has not witnessed it.

Daffron briefly considers overruling Binder and using an agency precede, perhaps with a two-column head, instead of the dictated insert.

Siegel is against it. "If.we are going to keep a man on the scene," he argues, "we must accept his judgment until it is proved wrong."

"I guess you're right," Daffron concedes.

Siegal prepares Binder's insert as a sub for the bracketed Reuters paragraph and works the phrase "Roadblock Put Up" into the existing one-column headline.

• • •

The updating on the fighting in Saigon, filed by Terry Smith six hours earlier, staggers into the New York wire room shortly before 3 o'clock. Not having heard from Smith, the foreign desk has used agency copy in late editions on the overnight action in Vietnam. Now there is not time to revamp Smith's story, much as Siegal would like to. Too bad. Smith will be disappointed, though not too much surprised, that the agencies got through ahead of him.

• • •

At two minutes before 3 o'clock, Siegal's phone rings. It's Dana Adams Schmidt, awash in Turkish coffee. Almost three hours have passed since the operator in Beirut instructed him to stand by for the call to New York. At one point in the wait, when the operator conceded "there will be a delay," he had risked driving his son to school. Now the call has come through.

"We're on deadline," Siegal tells him. "Can you give me something quick?" Schmidt dictates a couple of paragraphs. Siegal cuts him off. "That's all we have time for."

He shoots it to the composing room, without much hope that it will make the edition. It doesn't.

· · · · · · · · · · · · 3 a.m.

The Cleanup edition is locked up. But there is no "Good night"—not yet.

The skeleton crew in the newsroom—less than a dozen men—will sit out the deathwatch on Ike until 3:45 A.M.

At 3:08, the presses are signaled to a stop. The 50,000 copies of the Cleanup edition still to be printed will not be run off until it is clear there will be no further postscript. It will take only a few minutes to complete the run once the red start-the-press signal is flashed.

Nothing to do now but wait.

Copyboys wrap the day's accumulation of original copy into huge, neatly labeled bundles to be placed in storage bins and held for two weeks. It's the evidence—incontrovertible —in case of a libel suit or a serious factual error.

The deskmen type out brief memos for their day editors, filling them in on the night's activities.

"A quiet night with few significant changes or developments," Dick Roberts writes to Metropolitan Editor Arthur Gelb.

Daryl Frazell tells National News Editor Gene Roberts: "Shaw verdict fronted for two-thirty A.M. postscript. Otherwise quiet. Ike alive."

At 3:15, an Associated Press bulletin drops on Siegal's

desk. It says: THE AUTOBAHN, CLOSED FOR TWO HOURS THIS MORNING, HAS BEEN REOPENED.

Binder had been right.

Siegal and Daffron feel somewhat ashamed at having doubted their man on the spot. It is too late to get the new A.P. copy into the paper, but it does not matter. The story is nicely, and correctly, covered, thanks to Binder's cautious treatment.

Siegal turns his attention to the men who have been at the other end of the telephone and cable through the night. He answers their unasked questions: How did their stories fare?

• • •

Half a world away, in Vietnam, Terry Smith prepares to leave The Times's bureau at 203 Tu-Do on the main street of Saigon to attend the daily afternoon military briefing of correspondents. In his hand is a cable, just in from Siegal: YOUR INSERT WAR WHICH ARRIVED 2.40 A.M. NEW YORK TIME UNUSED. He will have to work last night's late combat details into today's story.

In Beirut, Dana Adams Schmidt is pumping his Arab sources for further details on the state of affairs in Syria and wondering how much of what he has already sent to New York got in the paper. A cable from Siegal tells him: THANKS FOR SYRIA STORY WHICH WENT BEYOND AGENCIES AND FRONTED THIRD EDITION DISPLACING REUTERS. Then, mindful of his conversation with Topping a couple of hours earlier, Siegal adds: KNOW YOU'LL TRY FOR TOMORROW'S PAPER TO PROVIDE FURTHER INTERPRETATION ON CAUSES OF TAKEOVER PLUS LIKELY EFFECTS ON SYRIAN POLICY.

In Berlin, David Binder sinks into an ancient leather-covered easy chair in The Times's bureau. He hopes New York heeded his advice and didn't overplay the blockade. Siegal's cable reassures him: YOUR INSERT USED FINAL EDITION AS THIRD PARAGRAPH OF UNICOL LEAD DIS-

PLACING REUTERS BRACKET. NOT REPEAT NOT
ABLE TO USE LATER AGENCIES REPORTING SHUT-
DOWN LIFTED BOTH ENDS AUTOBAHN.

Good—they listened to him. He's glad Siegal mentioned
that the lifting of the blockade did not make the paper. It will
guide him in framing his story today.

• • •

The day is ending very much as it began.

In the London wire room, at 9 o'clock, the first message of
the morning, for relay to New York, comes in. TOPPING
RETURNED DELHI LELYVELD.

Joseph Lelyveld is informing Topping that he is back in
New Delhi after his visit to Pakistan. As his message leaps
across the world, Lelyveld is at his typewriter, shades drawn
against India's broiling noonday sun, pecking away at the first
takes of a piece about the decline and fall of Mohammad
Ayub Khan.

Clive Barnes sits with his wife in the kitchen of their Manhattan apartment discussing, over a Scotch, the theatrical happening they have just witnessed at Fillmore East. The fantas-
tic rock groups went on and on into the early morning.
Maybe there's a piece in it for him; in their best moments
rock concerts approach pure theater. He'll think about it after
he gets some sleep, as soon as his eardrums stop vibrating.

John Canaday, after an exhausting eighteen-hour round of
ceremonies commemorating the fiftieth anniversary of the
Dayton Art Institute, comes suddenly awake in his hotel
room. Insomnia again. He jots down a few notes he wants to
be sure to include in his report of the program. He's booked
on an early morning plane to New York. He checks his 5 A.M.
call with the hotel operator, and dozes off.

• • •

In the 43d Street newsroom, porters have swept away much of
the debris. They now wait to move into the desk area where
the late crew still keeps the watch.

Al Blayer and Ray Cooper from the production department stand in the bullpen with Daffron, fingers crossed. They are waiting to give the pressroom full-speed-ahead instructions for the last 50,000 papers.

It's 3:40. If there is no word of Eisenhower's death in the next five minutes, the last of the trucks will be able to pull away shortly after 4 A.M., the overtime bills will be low and, most important, there won't be complaints about late deliveries.

At 3:43, Daffron sends a copyboy to make a last-minute check on the Associated Press and United Press International wires. They are clear.

At 3:44, Blayer dials the pressroom. "Put up the red light," he tells the foreman. The presses wind up.

At 3:45, the eyes of the dozen editors, rewrite men, clerks and copyboys rivet on Daffron. From behind his desk he calls across the floor:

"Good night!"

A Glossary
of Newspaper Terms

A-matter. Material that can be written in advance, before the lead develops; sometimes called B-matter, or Lede to kum.

Bank. Steel table on which pages are made up in composing room; also called Stone.

Banner. Eight-column head on page 1; also called Streamer.

Beat. Scene a reporter covers regularly, as Police Headquarters or City Hall.

Binder. Line at top of an inside page that binds together related stories.

Blockbuster. An extra large Takeout (*which see*).

B-matter. See A-matter.

Bulldog. First, or City, edition.

Bullpen. Desks of news editor and his assistants, which at one time were enclosed by a low wooden fence.

C.G.O. Can go over. Filler material, also called Plug, Punk, Reserve News, When Room.

Chase. Metal form in which a page is made up in the composing room; also called Form.

Close. Time at which a page is locked up in composing room; process of putting pages to bed, as "a good close" (pages went smoothly).

Crop. Eliminate insignificant or distracting elements of a picture to emphasize the significant portion.

Dead. Ad or story that has been used, or is not to be used.

Deadline. Closing time; last possible moment at which a story, picture or ad can be accepted for publication.

Dummy. Piece of paper ruled into columns to simulate a newspaper page and on which placement of ads and stories is indicated; used as guide by printer making up page; also called Scratch Sheet.

Ear. One of the small boxes at either side of the name plate at the top of page 1; one containing weather report, the other, the Times's slogan.

Exclusive. A story no other paper has.

Flag line. Name plate, or Logo, at the top of page 1.

Folio. The page number.

Folo. Story that follows another; also second-day story; *see Shirt-tail.*

Form. See Chase.

Fronting. Cable sent by The Times to foreign correspondents, informing them how their stories are played in the paper.

Future. Story that can be held over.

Galley. Shallow metal tray with upright sides to hold type.

Good night. Notification by the editor in charge that the operation is closed for the night.

Hed to kum. Copy editor's mark on story to inform composing room that headline will follow; almost always abbreviated to HTK.

Hellbox. Receptacle into which printer throws damaged or discarded type.

Jump. Continuation of a story from another page.

Justify. To align a page of type so that it will lock up securely.

Kicker. A line above, and at left, of main headline; also a bold-face lead-in to a picture caption.

Kill. Not to be used, as dead copy.

Lead. The opening portion of a story.

Lede to kum. Copy editor's mark on a story to inform composing room that lead will follow.

Live. Ready to use, not dead, as live copy.

Lobster shift. The shift that works from midnight to morning; genesis unknown.

Lock up. Tightening the quoins on a chase to lock the type firmly in place.

Logo. Name plate, or Flag line, at top of page 1.

Masthead. Box at top of editorial page, giving name and ownership of paper and listing principal officers and editors.

Mat. A papier-mâché replica of a page of type, from which a curved metal plate is cast.

Morgue. Department where clippings from the paper are filed.

New lead. Substitute introduction to a story.

News hole. Space set aside in the paper for everything but advertising.

Overnight. Assignment given out at night to cover something that will happen next day.

Overset. Stories written and set in type, but not printed.

Pad. Increase in number of copies to be printed, generally because of an unusual news development.

Pi. Lines of type that have been jumbled; out of normal sequence.

Plug. See C.G.O.

Postscript. Amended edition, as opposed to a new edition; interruption of press run to make correction or insert late news.

Punk. See C.G.O.

Put to bed. Close the pages in the composing room.

Q-head. The Times's term for a news analysis piece rather than a straight news story.

Replate. See Postscript.

Reserve News. See C.G.O.

Ribbon. A headline three or more columns wide.

Rim. Positions occupied by copyreaders at horseshoe-shaped copydesks.

Scratch sheet. See Dummy.

Second front. First page of second section; also called Split Page.

Shirttail. Story appended to another; a Folo.

Short. A brief story, rarely more than four paragraphs.

Sidebar. Separate story alongside the main story.

Slot. Position occupied by the head of the copydesk.

Slug. Word or label used to identify news copy.

Split page. See Second front.

Spread. A story longer than a Short (*which see*).

Starter. The last page to close in the composing room; so-called because when the starter plate is locked on the press cylinder, the press run starts.

Stone. See Bank.

Streamer. See Banner.

Stringer. Part-time correspondent, so called because he used to be paid by the number of words he wrote and his words, as printed, were pasted up and measured by a string. Other methods of payment are usually used now.

Sub. Substitute one piece of copy for another.

Subhead. Boldface line used to break up long stretch of type, or to introduce a new subject; also used to introduce a Shirttail.

Take. One section of a news story.

Takeout. A comprehensive story bringing up to date or explaining a given subject.

Turtle. A wheeled metal table on which page forms are carried from composing room make-up stones to stereotype mat machines.

When room. See C.G.O.

Widow. A short line ending a paragraph.

Wrap-up. A story that ties together all the loose ends, and gives all the latest information.

Index

The New York Times

© 1969 The New York Times Company.

LATE CITY EDITION

Weather: Partly sunny today. Cloudy
and seasonable tonight, tomorrow.
Temp. range: today 41-29; Friday
41-30. Full U.S. report on Page 62.

VOL. CXVIII..No. 40,579

NEW YORK, SATURDAY, MARCH 1, 1969

10 CENTS

NIXON, IN FRANCE, CALLS FOR AN END TO 'OLD QUARRELS'

De Gaulle Greeting Is Warm—Presidents Meet 2 Hours in 'Cordial' Discussion

MORE TALKS DUE TODAY

Exchange of Views to Cover Wide Range of Subjects, Including the Mideast

Texts of de Gaulle and Nixon statements are on Page 3.

By ROBERT B. SEMPLE Jr.
Special to The New York Times

PARIS, Feb. 28—Calling for an end to "old slogans" and "old quarrels," President Nixon arrived in France today for the last and most difficult phase of his eight-day diplomatic effort to repair the worn fabric of the North Atlantic alliance.

In a day of intensive conferences with Italian leaders in Rome, the President and his entourage flew to Orly Airport, touching down in the early afternoon to begin more than two days of ceremony and substantive discussions with President de Gaulle and other French officials.

Mr. Nixon regards his visit here as perhaps the most delicate stage of his tour, which has already led him to Brussels, London, Bonn, Berlin and Rome.

To Narrow Differences

Specifically, the hopes to begin tentative, low-key efforts to narrow outstanding dif-

---

SIRHAN PLEA TO DIE IS DENIED BY COURT

Judge Rejects Request After Jordanian Tries to Admit Guilt on All Charges

By DOUGLAS ROBINSON
Special to The New York Times

LOS ANGELES, Feb. 28—In a voice seething with anger, Sirhan B. Sirhan interrupted his

---

Eisenhower Is 'Weaker' As Pneumonia Develops

By FELIX BELAIR Jr.
Special to The New York Times

WASHINGTON, Feb. 28—lists that postponement of the
Former President Dwight D. operation would risk an intes-
Eisenhower suffered a serious tinal rupture and a gangrenous
setback today in his convales- condition of the intestinal tract.
cence from major abdominal The patient's intestinal stop-
surgery. The doctors decided page became progressively for
he had developed pneumonia in days when the doctors decided
his right lung. to operate on Sunday night.

A medical bulletin issued at
A bulletin on Monday said
Walter Reed Army Hospital call today for

CONFER AT ELYSÉE PALACE: President Nixon and President de Gaulle posing yesterday in Paris. They talked for more than two hours, alone except for interpreters, and are to meet today for lunch in Versailles and dinner in Paris.
United Press International

POLLUTION CURBS PRESSED BY HICKEL

He Calls for Stiffer Laws to Protect Offshore Water— Plan Praised in Senate

By WILLIAM M. BLAIR
Special to The New York Times

WASHINGTON, Feb. 28— Secretary of the Interior Wal-

G.I.'S BATTLE FOE ON EDGE OF SAIGON IN DAY-LONG CLASH

Enemy Found 6 Miles From Center of the Capital— Offensive Slows Further

By TERENCE SMITH
Special to The New York Times

SAIGON, South Vietnam, Feb 28—Enemy gunners shelled about 30 military and civilian targets around South Vietnam today while five combined American and South Vietnamese forces fought a day-long battle six miles from the center of Saigon.

The infantrymen were trying to encircle a force of North Vietnamese and Vietcong soldiers, estimated at 100 men, concealed in high brush in a swampy area near the village of Loiu, northeast of the capital.

It was the first time an enemy unit had maneuvered that close to Saigon in six months.

Elsewhere in the country, the enemy's six-day-old offensive dragged on at a considerably subdued pace. The shellings were generally lighter today and scattered.

Attacks Diminish

On Sunday, the first day of the current series of attacks, the enemy struck simultaneously with rocket and mortar fire at military and civilian areas. The attacks slowed to half of their original pace for the next several days and diminished even further yesterday.

U.S. Voices Concern On Berlin to Soviet

By BENJAMIN WELLES
Special to The New York Times

WASHINGTON, Feb. 28— The United States expressed its concern to the Soviet Union today about what appeared to be a mounting Soviet and East German campaign to impede access to West Berlin.

Under Secretary of State Elliot L. Richardson took the occasion of his first visit from Ambassador Anatoly F. Dobrynin to draw attention to press reports of a new Soviet note to the East German Government. Mr. Dobrynin's visit, from 4 to 4:30 P.M., had earlier been described as a courtesy call on the new Under Secretary.

The Soviet note alleged that West Germany was recruiting soldiers in West Berlin for its armed forces and was also procuring military

Continued on Page 6, Column 1

PRAGUE REJECTS A 'DICTATED UNITY'

Party Paper Terms Concept of Blind Obedience to Moscow 'Outdated'

By JONATHAN RANDAL
Special to The New York Times

PRAGUE, Feb. 28—The Czechoslovak Communist party newspaper today condemned the concept of world Communist unity. It implicitly rejected the doctrine of "limited sovereignty" that the Soviet Union enunciated last year to

---

NEW BERLIN CURBS BACKED BY SOVIET; ROADBLOCK PUT UP

Moscow Bids East Germans Restrict the Shipment of Industrial Products

ARMS FLOW IS ALLEGED

Warsaw Pact Commander Confers With Ulbricht— Mayor Urges Calm

The text of the Soviet note is printed on Page 4.

By DAVID BINDER
Special to The New York Times

BERLIN, Saturday, March 1 —The Soviet Union and its ally, East Germany, threatened last night to impose restrictions on traffic on the lifeline access routes between West Berlin and West Germany.

The warning was issued shortly after 8 o'clock last night, five hours after Marshal Ivan I. Yakubovsky of the Soviet Union, commander of the Warsaw Pact military forces, flew to East Berlin.

This morning, East German troops blocked the main Berlinbound autobahn at Marienborn, its western entry point. They erected a metal barrier and stationed armed guards, stopping traffic. It appeared possible, however, that the measure was connected with forthcoming Soviet-bloc military maneuvers in the area and would be only temporary.

Arms Production Alleged